THE ART OF
ReSILIENCE

A Life, Repurposed Compilation

THE ART OF
INSPIRING ESSAYS BY WOMEN

ReSILIENCE
ON LIFE AFTER HARD THINGS

MICHELLE RAYBURN
AND FRIENDS

The Art of Resilience
Copyright ©2026 Michelle Rayburn

ISBN: 978-1-954576-10-0
Published by Faith Creativity Life Books (FCL Books)
www.fclbooks.com

All rights reserved. No part of this publication may be reproduced, distributed, or transmitted in any form or by any means, including photocopying, recording, or other electronic or mechanical methods, without the prior written permission of the publisher, except in the case of brief quotations embodied in critical reviews and certain other noncommercial uses permitted by copyright law.

Some names have been changed to protect identities.

Unless otherwise indicated, Scripture quotations are taken from the Holy Bible, New Living Translation, copyright ©1996, 2004, 2015 by Tyndale House Foundation. Used by permission of Tyndale House Publishers, a Division of Tyndale House Ministries, Carol Stream, Illinois 60188. All rights reserved.

Compiled and edited by Michelle Rayburn – michellerayburn.com
Cover, typesetting, and ebook design by Michelle Rayburn
missionandmedia.com

Even though the fig trees have no blossoms,
and there are no grapes on the vines;
even though the olive crop fails,
and the fields lie empty and barren;
even though the flocks die in the fields,
and the cattle barns are empty,
yet I will rejoice in the Lord!

HABAKKUK 3:17-18

Contents

Foreword - xi

Faith

Granny Fitness and Grown-Up Faith - - - - - - - - - - - 3
  Michelle Rayburn

My First Real House - - - - - - - - - - - - - - - - - 9
  Kelly Wilson Mize

Change Doesn't Come Easily - - - - - - - - - - - - - 15
  Kathy Carlton Willis

Waterfalls and Wheelies - - - - - - - - - - - - - - 23
  Lisa-Anne Wooldridge

A Hundred Tiny Surrenders - - - - - - - - - - - - - 31
  Andrea M. Polnaszek, LCSW

When a Few Words Matter - - - - - - - - - - - - - - 37
  Joni Topper

The Step After the Pause - - - - - - - - - - - - - - 43
  Brooke R. Hackman

I Didn't Sign Up for This - - - - - - - - - - - - - - - - - 49
Lori Vober

For Such a Time - 55
Maureen Miller

Words Enough for Today - - - - - - - - - - - - - - - - 63
Heather Vogler

Courage

The Step That Changed Everything - - - - - - - - - - - 71
Tasha Schuh

Different Doesn't Mean Disordered - - - - - - - - - - - 79
Lisa L. Crowe

Faith Without a Safety Net - - - - - - - - - - - - - - - 85
Andrea Gribble

A Bold Move - 91
Mel Tavares

What Grows Underground - - - - - - - - - - - - - - - 99
Michelle Rayburn

Wearing "No" Like a Badge - - - - - - - - - - - - - - 107
Martha Knight

Five Words - 115
Crystal Stallman

Hair Today, Gone Tomorrow? - - - - - - - - - - - - - 121
Kathy Carlton Willis

Burnout Was the Breaking Point - - - - - - - - - - - - 129
Diana Leagh Matthews

Anchored in His Presence - - - - - - - - - - - - - - - - 137
Almira Michele Robinson

Love

God's Intentional Interruption - - - - - - - - - - - - - - 147
Joni Topper

From Tattoo to Titanium - - - - - - - - - - - - - - 155
Charlaine Martin

Hope After Hurt - - - - - - - - - - - - - - - - - - 161
Alisa O'Donnell

Big-Time Trouble - - - - - - - - - - - - - - - - - 169
Sue Ferguson

Courage When Lights Go Out - - - - - - - - - - - - 175
Kay Nell Miller

Perfectly Stationed - - - - - - - - - - - - - - - - - 181
Pam Whitley Taylor

Waiting at the Window - - - - - - - - - - - - - - - 187
Paula Hemingway

After the Harvest - - - - - - - - - - - - - - - - - - 195
Michelle Rayburn

About the Contributors - - - - - - - - - - - - - - - 201

Foreword

WE OFTEN RECOGNIZE RESILIENCE IN others, but it takes shape more quietly in the middle of ordinary days. Until the hardest chapters come, our stories might even seem mundane. But the call to start over, try again, or walk an impossible path invites the kind of grit we didn't know was beneath the surface.

The women in this book are strong. Their stories carry depths I have not walked myself. Through their lived experiences, we see the kind of honesty and courage that inspires us when we need the voices of others who have been there before.

This is not a how-to guide or a promise of neat resolutions. If you're holding this book, your story is still being written—ours are too. And we offer companionship rather than a pattern to model. If you're reading from a place of weariness or rebuilding, on the inside of uncertainty or discouragement, we see you.

I've had the honor of gathering and curating the essays—and writing a few of my own. Now, as these women have entrusted me with their stories, I present them to you, hoping you'll recognize pieces of your own journey within ours.

May our words meet you where you are and remind you that even slow and imperfect growth matters.

Before you turn the page, may I pray for you?

Prayer:

God, you are the original Artist.

You have been present with every story in these pages, and you're present in the story still being written in the life of the one holding this book. You know each place of weariness, the named losses and the ones still unspoken, the victories and the disappointments.

I pray that you would bring comfort where hearts are tender and courage where fear overwhelms. Teach patience in the slow work of becoming. May resilience take form in honest, imperfect, and beautiful ways on this canvas, a masterpiece in progress. And may love be the truest mark of your signature on what is still being shaped. Amen.

Happy reading to you! I hope you'll consider us friends by the time you finish.

Michelle

Faith

Granny Fitness and Grown-Up Faith

MICHELLE RAYBURN

I HAD BEEN TALKING ABOUT BUILDING more muscle for months, but I was all talk and no action. The hand weights stayed tucked away in a footstool storage compartment, a convenient way to avoid them—out of sight, out of mind. But then, a friend, who had taken fitness accountability to a level that matched actual accountability, texted me a picture of an ad about a free class that a local clinic was sponsoring at the fitness center in my community.

The description said, "This multi-week evidence-based strength training program is designed for middle-aged and older women and men. Each class includes progressive weight training, flexibility and balance activities." It sounded perfect for my mid-forties needs.

Did I mention the class was free? Twice a week at the gym, where other people *pay* for memberships. For free. I don't really like group workouts, but this seemed doable. And I'm a sucker for a good bargain.

There were two options: regular and advanced.

I decided I should do the regular. After all, I had no idea what I was doing and had no business calling myself advanced in any area of fitness.

But, as I thought about it more, I decided I should probably get more details. Just what did *advanced* entail? Was there a list of criteria somewhere?

It turned out the qualification for the advanced class was that I could get up off the floor without assistance. I was *so* winning at this physical fitness thing.

Slow-Motion Reps

I arrived at 9:00 a.m. in the aerobics room of the fitness center. Others were already there with their hand weights selected and yoga mats rolled out. I found a spot and glanced around the room. I think it was fair to assume I was the youngest person in the class, based on hair color alone. And since the friend who had suggested the class had conveniently not signed up, I was all by myself.

> Somehow, I had joined granny fitness.

Somehow, I had joined granny fitness.
I am SO going to ace this class. Bring it on!
So far, I was burning most of my calories by rolling my eyes.
We started our workout with slow-motion squats.
Pshaw! Slow motion?
This is the point at which you can probably see the arrogance I somehow missed. I'm obtuse like that sometimes. And never underestimate grannies.

The instructor reminded us that this motion would build the muscles we needed to get up and down from a chair safely. She explained that plopping into a chair with a giant whoosh wasn't good for our bodies.

What does she know?

Never mind how many times I whooshed into my office chair every day and how many times I grunted my way back out.

Our slow-motion squats began from a seated position on a chair, and we slowly rose.

"Up, two, three, four . . ."

And then we gradually lowered.

" . . . Down, two, three, four," the instructor counted.

After a brief tap of the tushy on the chair, we started the next rep.

Up, two, three, four, and so on.

Before the end of the second set of reps began, the class was already kicking my behind. Not the old ladies. They were super sweet. The workout.

Several exercises kicked me in the patootie. Right between the gluteus medius and gluteus maximus, I felt it.

Or maybe it was the gluteus minimus.

Whatever.

But then we did this heel-to-tippy-toes maneuver that made my right ham hock start to tremble. For a thirty-second eternity, I stayed on tiptoes, while the cuff of my yoga capris quivered quite noticeably. As we continued those reps, I hoped none of the grannies noticed this solid evidence of ineptitude.

> I hoped none of the grannies noticed this solid evidence of ineptitude.

Then, we did wrist exercises to "help us with the dexterity to operate a can opener" and overhead reaches to improve our coordination for getting things out of the cupboard. Some exercises were to strengthen the muscles that would make us less prone to falls. I came face-to-face with the impending challenges of older adulthood while the workout shredded my pride.

When I arrived home, I could hardly lift my thighs high enough to ascend the stairs to my main living area. In fact, I almost tripped and fell. Which I found to be a little ironic—since the purpose of the class and such. I moved around like someone eighty-eight instead of forty-eight for a few days before going back for more granny fitness.

Comparison Versus Conditioning

I've noticed that faith and fitness are a lot alike. There's so much comparison in life, isn't there? We look around and decide who is advanced in their spiritual growth and pre-judge who we think isn't.

Who seems to recover quickly after a loss.

Who prays with ease or has just the right words to say all the time.

Who gets back up with seemingly no effort after life kicks them down.

Who doesn't appear to shake when their faith is tested and stretched.

> Spiritual strength can't be assumed by appearances any more than physical strength can.

But spiritual strength can't be assumed by appearances any more than physical strength can. It isn't a competition or comparison but a conditioning. It's fast to make a comparison, but the conditioning comes slowly.

Things like grief have a way of exposing our vulnerability and opening a window for comparison. We know others—or maybe it's ourselves—who can't find their footing quickly when grief knocks them over. Where every day is like trudging through loose sand. The distorted idea that grief has a beginning and an end is no different from assuming muscle tone has a point of achievement or arrival rather than being an ongoing conditioning process. Grief doesn't come with an expiration date or an itinerary.

> We don't all train in the same season or at the same pace.

Similarly, trouble shows up when we least expect it, bringing trials that seem insurmountable. Health challenges, pain, loss, broken relationships, trauma, and disruptions. Each experience forms us. We don't all train in the same season or at the same pace. Some of us discover we need more practice than we realized. I know this quite well when something shakes my faith. But it isn't failure. It is formation. I can honestly say I have grown from every challenge I've faced.

Some of us discover resilience we never knew we had.

Our common ground with one another is that we work with the body we have. With the life we have. The circumstances we have. God shows up as we develop faith muscles through repetition. And repetition is painful.

When we compare to others, we ask, "Why am I not where they are?"

But when we frame every situation as faith conditioning, we can ask, "What is God strengthening in *me* right now?"

Slow-Motion Faith

This life we're in is not a bodybuilding competition or a race. And growing resilience isn't glamorous. It's a lot like the slow-motion squats that seem too small to make a difference at first glance—or first squat. But each repetition is a movement that matters. Showing up again after disappointment. Saying the hard thing and processing the lingering awkwardness. Sitting with the unanswered questions. Learning to be curious instead of prescribing "you shoulds" for everyone else.

We like resolution and neatly wrapped endings. But it's slower and steadier than that. I've often assumed that the ones who appear strong must have been spared the struggle, until I hear their stories. Mind-blowing tales of unimaginable hardship. Abuse. Heartbreak. Unspeakable things. It turns out, their grit wasn't easily acquired. Repetition and patience led the way as the struggle lingered, and often still lingers.

Now, when my eyes drift to someone else's corner, it isn't to compare but to commiserate. To cheer, console, and to empathize. God is at work among us. This is about all of us doing the steady work of becoming resilient together.

My First Real House

KELLY WILSON MIZE

IT WAS MY FIRST REAL house. Up until I was fifteen years old, my parents were deeply involved in a ministry that often required us to switch houses every few years. Just as I would get used to one home, we would pack up and move to another. When my parents finally transitioned out of that ministry and settled into family property in my parents' hometown—a house once inhabited by my grandmother—I felt an unfamiliar thrill: a sense of permanence.

The house was far from glamorous. Simple and timeworn, yet shaped by family history, it felt like a new life to me. My parents worked hard to restore it, and I was delighted by the transformation. It was more than a place to sleep and eat—it was home. I loved my first real house so much that when I got married years later, I insisted on holding my wedding reception there. It might have been modest, but the house represented stability, belonging, and love.

My father was very handy and spent years shaping and reshaping the house around my mother's vision—sometimes making unusual or quirky improvements, but always with her wishes at the center. His handiwork became a quiet testimony of love and partnership. For decades after I got married, I cherished return trips to visit my parents. And my children? A Disney World vacation had nothing on a trip to visit their grandparents. That house stood like an anchor, a reminder that no matter how far life pulled us, there was a place where the foundation was familiar and secure.

Houses Age, and So Do We

Houses, like people, age. Time creeps in through the window frames and presses against the siding. Just as wrinkles appear on human faces, cracks occur on walls. Paint fades, memories grow heavier, and upkeep becomes relentless.

> I felt both comforted by memories and burdened by the evidence of time.

My parents aged alongside their house. Visits during those years became bittersweet. What was once a place of warmth and celebration began to carry the weight of decline. Each visit meant facing the slow, painful reality of my parents' fading strength. Walking through the familiar rooms, I felt both comforted by memories and burdened by the evidence of time. The house I had once claimed as my joyful refuge became a mirror of loss—home not only to my family's history, but also to the hard truth that the ones who made it a home were slipping away.

My father lived to be one week short of ninety-one. After he passed, the house seemed painfully quiet, almost as if it, too, was grieving. My brother and I helped our mother—delivering groceries, mowing the lawn, keeping up with bills and repairs—but the day came when she could no longer live alone. The house, once a joyful sanctuary, now felt like a heavy weight. Its needs outpaced our energy.

The question loomed: What do we do with the house? Keep it? Sell it? Preserve it somehow? The decision about what to do with our parents' home was never just about a house—it was about legacy, identity, and resilience.

Passing the Torch

Eventually, an answer emerged. My cousin and her husband wanted to buy the house, refurbish it, and claim the land our shared grandmother had cherished. It was not a transaction of strangers but a continuation of our family's story. Even more poignant, my widowed aunt—my father's sister—would live with her daughter and son-in-law there. Now in her nineties herself, she would return to a property that shaped many memories and even inhabit the same bedroom where my father spent his final days. The closeness of their sibling bond made this almost poetic—a circle closing, a restoration of place and relationship.

> I didn't fully realize how difficult it would be to go through the house, clean it out, and say goodbye.

I didn't fully realize how difficult it would be to go through the house, clean it out, and say goodbye. Each drawer, closet, and corner seemed to hold a piece of my parents' lives and mine—so many photos tucked away, handwritten notes, saved greeting cards, and page after page of Bible verses written out word for word by my mother.

In seventy-two years of marriage, I don't think my parents ever threw anything away! The kitchen overflowed with pots, pans, and multiple sets of every other imaginable kitchen supply. Each one bore the marks of decades spent selflessly preparing comforting meals for loved ones.

Looking at my father's vast library of books and collection of tools triggered an emotional response because I knew each one still bore his invisible fingerprints. I had predicted that the sheer amount of physical work of cleaning out the house would be daunting, but the emotional weight proved much heavier. Sorting through my parents' belongings felt like dismantling the very fabric of their story.

What could have been a practical task became a journey through memory, grief, and reluctant release. Sometimes resilience means letting go—and trusting that what truly matters can live on in a new form. Thankfully, the house, like our family, wasn't being abandoned; it was being given a chance to begin again.

Resilience in Renewal

Home renovation has become a cultural fascination, both on our screens and in real life. I think it's because we're drawn to the hope of renewal—the idea that what looks broken can be made whole again. Floors can be refinished, walls repainted, and roofs replaced. Even when neglected, the bones often remain strong. A structure may sag, leak, or crumble in places, but with care, it can be restored to stand again, usually even better than before.

> Resilience is not a flawless structure but trusting the one who builds unshakable foundations.

Like the house itself, the women who lived in the house illustrate resilience. My grandmother, the first in our family to live within its walls, endured hardship with dignity. My mother, after losing her husband, leaned on her children and faith to keep moving forward. My cousin, who would be the agent of welcome improvement for the house, and my aunt, who would embrace a new beginning late in life, show that God can plant some form of satisfaction in every chapter. And I, like them, continue to learn that resilience is not a flawless structure but trusting the one who builds unshakable foundations.

Seasons of growth and decline touch us all. We lose loved ones, face setbacks, and endure challenges that shake our sense of stability. Like old houses, we wear out with time, but that doesn't mean we can't be renewed. Just as a home can find new life through repair and care, people can discover fresh purpose in starting over. The cracks and imperfections of our past don't disappear, but they can become places where hope and strength shine through.

> The cracks and imperfections...can become places where hope and strength shine through.

My house story is one thread in a larger tapestry of those who embody resilience by starting over. Some do so by creating a new home from scratch. Others reinvent themselves after children are grown, returning to long-forgotten dreams. Still others learn resilience through loss—rebuilding after a death, divorce, or career change.

Like an old family home, people carry scars. Yet when given the chance to reimagine our lives, we become more than survivors—we become testimonies to the beauty of starting anew. Our resilience inspires because we trust God to bring us through storms.

The Legacy We Share

As my extended family builds from the foundation of the house their loved ones once inhabited, I see a living parable. The walls that once held laughter will now hear new conversations. The floors will support the weight of different footsteps while remaining steady.

The house stands, both old and new, weary but full of promise. So too, the women in my family stand. We carry memories and responsibilities, but also the hope of renewal. Because resilience is not pretending to be unbroken—it is believing that life, like an old house, can be lovingly restored.

My story is meaningful, but not unique. Many families pass down a home or property, and while the details differ, it's the weight of the history that matters. These places hold more than walls and furniture; they contain echoes of love, labor, sacrifice, and belonging. They remind us where we've come from and point us toward the legacies we are called to carry forward.

> They remind us where we've come from and point us toward the legacies we are called to carry forward.

From my first real house, I learned lessons that reach far beyond its walls. Resilience is one of many things I will carry with me. Strength is not perfection. True resilience is not found in houses that never age or in lives that never falter. It is found in the grace to let go, the courage to rebuild, and the beauty to begin again—with God's faithfulness as our only sure foundation.

Change Doesn't Come Easily

KATHY CARLTON WILLIS

IF YOU WANT TO TALK about resilience, all you have to do is look at Mom's address book under "W." I've pretty much taken over that section with thirty moves, mostly due to my husband's job as a pastor and chaplain. I joke that with my next address change, I'll send out new address pages, but thankfully, most of us use our phone's contacts app to update address changes now.

I understand the word *transplant* a lot better than the word *rooted*. That certainly sets a person up to either be resilient or resentful. And truthfully, there are times I waver from one to the other—only because desiring to be rooted is so deep in my soul. What I've figured out is that the ache I have from being a frequent transplant only means I'm homesick for heaven—a place I've never been, but where my true forever home will be. When I'm homesick, I can't really go home again. Too much has changed, and what I miss is no longer there. What I'm really longing for isn't a place, but a person. God. But a little bit of heaven on earth would be nice. I haven't found a CITY LIMIT or a NO TRESPASSING sign that can keep God out.

Abide

Until I experience being fully rooted, *abide* takes on a whole new meaning. Rather than looking for a home to abide in, I strive to abide in Christ. Remain. Dwell. Linger.

Abiding in the Vine gives me that sense of connection I long for. As I depend on Christ, I am sustained by him, nourished to be fruitful, and able to draw life—true life in Jesus—rather than merely existing in mundane rituals and routines.

> The safest home, where all the security systems work and the address doesn't matter, is making my home in Christ.

The safest home, where all the security systems work and the address doesn't matter, is making my home in Christ. When I sink my roots into his love, there is peace that fuels contentment. His presence beckons me to settle my soul in him and tether my heart to his. This is living from the Vine. (You know, I drive on Vine Avenue on my way to and from church. Now I'll look at that as a reminder to abide—a sign that Jesus is with me.)

Hard Things

The problem with moving often is enduring lots of hard things. Enduring—another form of resilience. For example, when I moved from Ohio to Texas, some in my new church family called me a "d--- Yankee," and yes, they meant it in a derogatory way.

When we moved to New Mexico, I realized deserts don't mix with dry eyes and contacts. It didn't do much for my dried-out heart either. At the time, I was still hurting from my husband being voted out of our last pastorate.

Starting over, and over, and over is no fun. Yes, it's an adventure in new spaces and places, but it's the opposite of feeling rooted. Moving means finding new doctors and new friends. I found out I pretty much stink at knowing who to trust with my heart. Sometimes, trusting others looks more like *guarding* your heart.

What Helped

Rather than staying focused on the negatives, I looked for the blessings. Finding a purpose in each place we lived. Starting over is a great opportunity to try out different careers and causes. Discovering a new friend. Trying out new home styles and architecture, from one hundred years old to a brand-new build, and everything in between. Looking for something beautiful in each region—its varied terrain, distinctive plants, and unique scenery.

Resilience looks like dusting off your sandals and moving on. It's not *really* starting over because you're taking with you all the experience you've gained, for the good and for the bad. Those experiences are what help us learn how to bounce back.

> A resilient person rebounds with their hope intact.

Bouncing Back

The ability to bounce back should be an Olympic sport. Now *that* would be an event where I'd take home the gold. I have plenty of jiggle to help with the bouncing, but it sounds rather painful. I guess most sports are! In the case of resilience, bouncing back describes a person's ability to recover from setbacks, adversity, and disappointments. Someone who gets knocked down but doesn't stay down—emotionally, mentally, spiritually, or physically. A resilient person rebounds with their hope intact.

It's not just bouncing back either; it's persevering with persistence—giving pushback when being gaslit rather than letting others walk all over us.

Resilience takes dogged determination. That makes me think of my Boston terrier, Hettie. She has definite signs of that. Some call it tenacity. Others call it stubborn. Either way, she makes sure she gets what she's after! It's fun watching her brain work. If plan A doesn't work, she immediately goes with plan B, without sulking or giving in. I want to be her when I grow up! Come to think of it, she has a pretty good life! Even when she's begging me for something, her persistence usually pays off.

Longevity of Belonging

I lived in the same house from the time I was born until the time I was married. I rarely left the county. Imagine the change that came. I'll never beat my nineteen-year record of living in my hometown with the same address. Well, maybe. But I'd have to live a long time in this condo. We bought it with "aging in place" in mind, but that would be stretching it. I'm guessing I'll be in a nursing home by that age. Age eighty. Hmmm . . . you never know. I do come from good aging genes. So, you heard it here first. I'm going to try to break my record for the longest time in one dwelling!

Don't get me wrong. Sometimes we have to quit in order to fight! We have to move on. We have to make a different choice to get a different outcome. But we'll never know what could have been if we give up.

Resilience Heroes

Resilient people overcome difficult circumstances and embrace change rather than begrudging the need for it. I'm inspired by my mom and many other strong women who came before me. They taught me from a young age how to be resilient.

Mom has reinvented her life several times. When she married my dad, she left behind some hard struggles and started over in a new state, knowing no one. At age forty, she started college and earned her RN degree. By age forty-six, she was a widow. She purchased a different home, and not long after that, moved to a nearby state. She moved a few times, and each time developed wonderful friendships and created the life she wanted to experience. When she retired, she moved to yet another state. She attended a volunteer expo to discover opportunities in town to serve. She became an award-winning Master Gardener and also served with Habitat for Humanity.

Even in her current senior community, she teaches gardening and cooking and helps with projects such as baking Christmas cookies for the residents of a nearby nursing home. Mom is the most resilient person I know.

My Grandma Mary was widowed at age thirty-two, and she had five living children at the time. She endured hardship through difficult winter months, even living in a tent with her family so they wouldn't be separated.

> The only way to know if you have resilience is to go through difficult circumstances. That's the only test of what a person has inside of them.

There have been others who have inspired me. They endured great hardship and overcame it by hoping for something better (or at least different) and then waking up each day to see what life might bring. As I went on a prayer walk today, I realized the only way to know if you have resilience is to go through difficult circumstances. That's the only test of what a person has inside of them. Will they give up or will they dig in and try again?

Sometimes we need to try longer at what we know is right, and other times we need to try something new. Either way, it's the endurance that gets us through the challenges.

Ruth and Naomi

I think about Ruth and Naomi in the Bible. They endured great hardship when their husbands died. Ruth was Naomi's daughter-in-law. In that culture, it left them both with no security, no heirs, and an uncertain future. Naomi blamed God for her loss and felt like the Lord had dealt bitterly with her. She decided to return home to Bethlehem and asked to be called Mara, a name meaning "bitter." She felt empty, yet full of bitterness.

> "Don't call me Naomi," she responded. "Instead, call me Mara, for the Almighty has made life very bitter for me. I went away full, but the Lord has brought me home empty. Why call me Naomi when the Lord has caused me to suffer and the Almighty has sent such tragedy upon me?" (Ruth 1:20–21)

In contrast, Ruth, her Moabite daughter-in-law, remained hopeful for a better outcome. Rather than staying with her own family, Ruth vowed to be loyal to Naomi and traveled with her to Naomi's homeland—leaving her own country behind. Ruth followed Naomi's instructions for redemption. In the process, she provided for them both, and ultimately, Naomi's heart softened again. The family line would one day lead to King David and, generations later, to Jesus. What a resiliency story!

Plan for It or Not?

Sometimes we plan, we plan, we plan, but then life intervenes! It seems part of resilience is learning to be flexible and pliable rather than set in our ways. But I can't help it, like that TV character Colonel John "Hannibal" Smith said, "I love it when a plan comes together!"*

I have neuroinflammation and am in a two-year neuro rehab program that teaches neuroplasticity. I'm amazed at how God has created our brains. Neuroplasticity is the brain's built-in ability to adapt, reroute, and create new pathways when something has impaired the old pathways of cognitive function.† Similarly, resilient people learn to adapt when life brings about a challenge not of our own choosing. Neuroscience has shown that when old pathways become blocked or damaged, the brain doesn't simply give up—it looks for another way. With training, it is able to build the capacity to do what once felt impossible.

> The brain doesn't simply give up—it looks for another way.

In the same way, resilient people learn to pivot rather than break, to rewrite the internal scripts that no longer serve them, and to practice new patterns until they become second nature. Neuroplasticity shows us that resilience isn't about being untouched by hardship—it's about the remarkable God-designed ability to grow, heal, and transform in response to it. Our brains are wired to learn, to adjust, and to find new ways forward. Our souls can do the same. That is resilience in action.

---

* A frequent reference from the character on NBC's *The A-Team* (1983–1986).
† "How Does Neuroplasticity Work?," National Institute for the Clinical Application of Behavioral Medicine (NICABM), accessed December 30, 2025, https://www.nicabm.com/brain-how-does-neuroplasticity-work/.

Resiliency Traits

Although change doesn't come easily, I had to start where I was to pick up new traits to help me become more resilient. Rather than succumbing to the temptation of blaming my personality or my circumstances, I learned new techniques for my mindset and choices. Figuring out next steps involved adapting, problem-solving, and discovering a sense of purpose. When I told God I was willing to try new things, he empowered me with the strength to do so. Instead of *neuroplasticity*, I guess it would be *soulplasticity*.

> Instead of *neuroplasticity*, I guess it would be *soulplasticity*.

Even though it took a lot to be intentional with changing my attitude and internal self-talk, it helped me adopt hopeful realism and reminded me to extend self-compassion. Sometimes we are so hard on ourselves! When our actions become more intentional, we create flexibility within healthy boundaries. Our spiritual roots deepen through centering prayers and staying grounded in our faith. And when we've done all that's ours to do, a sense of humor goes a long way!

Waterfalls and Wheelies

LISA-ANNE WOOLDRIDGE

I HELD TIGHT TO MY COUSIN'S hand at the crest of the falls. I already regretted the choice to be there on the brink, terrified to take the plunge. He didn't let go of my hand or push me over the edge. Instead, he took my other hand, so I was looking at him and not the blue-green pool below.

I've thought about that moment many times since—the impossible cornflower sky and the swift water coursing over my feet, the encouragement of rowdy friends cheering me on, the way my stomach dropped as we jumped, and the sheer adrenaline rush of cold water covering my head before we kicked our way to the surface. Even though the impact and current pushed us apart, my cousin was still right beside me, whooping as only a Kentucky boy can. Don't ask where our parents were; it was a different time—we looked out for each other with no parental supervision whatsoever.

Adventures in Derring-Do

One leap. That's all it took. It was a baptism in endorphins, and my brain was hooked on the dopamine high. I wasn't blessed with good sense, so my youth was full of things I'd ground my own kids over.

Once, I scaled a cliff that overhung the Ohio River to impress my younger cousins at a family reunion. I didn't get in trouble only because my grandpa reminded my dad he'd done exactly the same thing thirty years before. Another time, by myself, I explored a long-abandoned mine's air shaft to see what I could find—sadly, just coal, no gold.

> I would disappear for the whole day on my adventures.

I would disappear for the whole day on my adventures. One summer morning I walked for several hours into the woods near my home to eat blackberries and drink from a beautiful artesian well in the middle of an untouched glade. I wanted to live there forever! When the late-afternoon sun lit up the trunks of the trees, I realized I might have to live in the woods if I didn't get home on time. With a stitch in my side and shin splints, I skidded across the threshold just as the streetlights flickered on. I never told anybody about that, until now, because at nine years old, I wasn't even technically allowed to cross the street.

Adventures in Babysitting

The desire for new adventures only grew with each passing year. I took unusual jobs that let me do exciting things. Wild cave exploration, rescuing a group of people from a zip line in a lightning storm, bungee jumping dozens of times a day—I loved it all, and a part of me never wanted to grow up. I majored in recreation and outdoor education in college and worked for several youth camps. Anything that let me be outside having a good time seemed like a dream job. I trained in every skill I could—kayaking, wilderness survival, using a compound bow, environmental and nature study, and horseback riding.

I had an insatiable appetite to go, do, and be as much as possible. Throw in a group of little kids or middle schoolers to take on long hikes and overnight camping trips, and I wouldn't stop smiling for days. Later, after I was married, I worked as a youth minister, introducing teens to everything from wilderness adventures to interpretive dance routines. Those kids were up for anything, and so was I. When I wasn't chasing an adrenaline rush, I loved just being outside in nature, climbing trees, finding secluded beauty spots to dream, read, or pray. I took it for granted that this was my life, and it would always be this way.

> When I wasn't chasing an adrenaline rush, I loved just being outside in nature, climbing trees, finding secluded beauty spots to dream, read, or pray.

Adventures in Paradise

Things did change, though, as they inevitably do. My husband was offered a job in Silicon Valley halfway through grad school, and we both knew it was the right thing to do. He was a programmer just as the World Wide Web was catching on, and California was the place to be.

For me, it was paradise. Beautiful weather most of the year, and the bad weather was fantastic compared to the Midwest. We had endless outdoor playgrounds to explore, awe-inspiring redwood forests, breathtaking mountains, and the incomparable Pacific Ocean. I cried for a solid thirty minutes the first time I saw the redwoods and sat under one with my journal. I didn't write a thing, but my heart soared beyond the canopy of the thirty-story trees.

I learned all I could about the ocean. Even though it was bone-chilling cold at times, I never felt more alive than when I waded out past the breakers, dove into an oncoming wave, and let the powerful current push me back to shore. California was nature on steroids, and I'd never been happier. I had no idea that the next wave of adventure would nearly be a wipeout.

My sense of adventure carried into starting a family.

Adventures in Parenting

One minute, I was a pregnant, happy, active twenty-five-year-old. The next, I was the mother of a tiny twenty-eight-week-old preemie fighting for his life. The odds of surviving and thriving were stacked against him. We were far away from our families, very young, and without other support. Our church and friends from other churches stepped into the gap and prayed for months. I'm not sure where we'd be without their love and help.

> We had truly miraculous answers to prayer too. Yes, miraculous.

We had truly miraculous answers to prayer too. Yes, miraculous. When the doctor says, "I've never seen this before; it's a miracle," and the sweet mom from India asks you to have people pray for her tiny baby girl too, there's no argument. Before we left the NICU three months later, a group of mothers from all backgrounds were joining us in prayer, right in the heart of downtown San Francisco.

What followed were the hardest and best years of our lives. Medical crises followed one right after the other. Our baby's health was fragile, and I was put on medical bedrest with our second child just over a year later. Our son was frequently hospitalized—an average cold could make his tiny throat swell shut or cause his delicate lungs to be overwhelmed. He had many challenges to overcome, from being premature, requiring medical specialists and long-term physical and developmental therapies. By the time we had our third child—ten years later and another six months of bedrest for me—he had defied all his diagnoses. I'd call that season more of an odyssey than an adventure, but it felt like a roller coaster either way!

Somewhere in the middle of all that chaos, I homeschooled all three children. I wasn't sure how that happy adventure would work out, but with a lot of grace and help from the Lord, it did. I got to share my love of outdoor adventures with my children—seeing them play in the snow at Yosemite or swim and canoe on Lake Tahoe or wade up a stream in the Santa Cruz redwoods filled my cup to running over. Watching them earn honors in their university studies and choose their own paths in life does my heart a world of good.

As they grew up, however, I found myself facing a whole new set of adventures, but certainly not the kind I was after.

Adventures in Sitting Down

In my mid-forties I'd started having health issues, but I was too busy to worry much about it. I'd inherited some conditions, like a thyroid that refused to work properly and some familial cholesterol concerns, but I was determined not to let anything slow me down or stop me from fully enjoying my life. That attitude worked well for me, until it didn't.

> I was determined not to let anything slow me down or stop me from fully enjoying my life.

Injuries began piling up, and new diagnoses popped up faster than a pan of Jiffy Pop on a campfire. The hardest part was how powerless I felt. The doctors had very few answers other than,

"Lose a few pounds," or "Would you like a prescription for pain medication?" I knew neither of those things would fix the problems, but it seemed like every part of my body was under attack in one way or another.

> It seemed like every part of my body was under attack in one way or another.

I was a tough guy about it all and tried just to carry on so I could be there for my family and continue to do the things I loved. But as fast as I tried to outrun it, the pain grew and slowed me down more and more. All the procedures, medications, and specialists did little to help. My family and friends watched helplessly as my world began to shrink. I took refuge in the online world, where I made many wonderful friends. Most of them have no idea of the struggles I face, and for a long time, I preferred it that way. But as things have progressed, it feels less helpful and not honest to hide my pain from people who care about me.

Adventures in Wonderland

Three years ago, we moved from the Bay Area of California to a small town in Oregon, trading an upstairs townhouse for a single-level home. It's much safer for me and has room for my mobility aids. Since we've been here, people have been very kind and quick to help with anything I need, and the city council is working hard to make our historic downtown more accessible for everyone. I used to be stubbornly independent and loved to help other people, but now I'm on the opposite side, learning to receive it.

One verse I love talks about God preparing our paths. I have no doubt this is true! Even though we left behind everything familiar and people we dearly love, God knows what he's doing. I suspect our real estate agent was a plant from heaven's home office because we traded paradise for wonderland. We are surrounded by mountains and trees, lakes and rivers, and that's just in town. The wildness and beauty of this place have to be experienced to be believed.

The hardest thing for me, though, is that much of the beauty is just out of reach. My condition has worsened, and I'm in a wheelchair most of the time. I can't just walk out my door, greet the sunshine, and take a long hike. I can't walk on the sand or dip my toes in the ocean. I can't play in the snow or pick my way down to the creek bed to hunt for agates. For a while, it threatened to crush my soul altogether to realize that I just wasn't getting better and that I was missing out on so much. But that's not the end of my story.

I may never get better, but I have reason to hope. New answers, new therapies, and new medicines to try. An old family creed of ours is *Dum spiro spero*, which translates from Latin as, "While I breathe, I hope." Hope gives me strength and helps me rebound from discouragement. It reminds me to celebrate every good thing and to really see the beauty close at hand. When I allow faith and hope to combine, I see endless new possibilities waiting for me. And in the meantime, you'll find me on one of the ever-increasing accessible trails, picnic grounds, or beach mats that the state of Oregon and my own little town are investing in.

> When I allow faith and hope to combine, I see endless new possibilities.

I'll have my adventures and maybe even pop a wheelie or two in my wheelchair. I may have a hard life for now, but I have a good God, and with him, the adventures are never-ending.

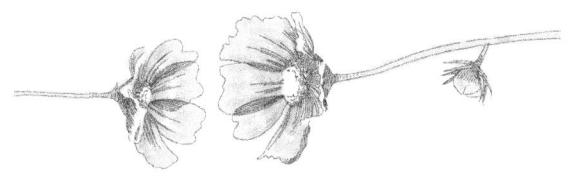

A Hundred Tiny Surrenders

ANDREA M. POLNASZEK, LCSW

I WAS DRIVING OUR THOUSAND-DOLLAR CHEVY down the interstate, headed to my first day as a therapist, when a loud bang erupted, and smoke poured from the hood. I coasted into the breakdown lane; the car was dead. I could see the exit ramp and the McDonald's sign lit up about half a mile ahead.

I did the only thing I could. I began to walk. This car was old. I was grateful that it worked, but it didn't have any bells or whistles. There was no interior temperature gauge, so I didn't know that I should be nervous about the weather.

A white Cadillac pulled over next to me. Every instinct screamed, "Don't get in a car with a stranger."

Then the woman rolled down her window and said softly, "Please let me drive you. It's twenty-five below today."

Something shifted inside me. I wasn't dressed for a long walk in subzero temperatures. Suddenly, I thought the risk that she might hurt me was outweighed by the idea that I might get frostbite. I climbed into the back seat.

We made mindless chit-chat while she drove. Soon, she delivered me safely to the warm glow of those golden arches. I bought coffee with shaking hands. Then I called my husband, Perry, and a tow truck.

That morning felt like rock bottom, but it was actually a hinge on which the door of my life swung open. It ended up being a pivot point for a new beginning.

Changing Gears

Six months earlier, I had been living a dream in reverse. My sister, brother-in-law, and I co-wrote a screenplay based on my book *The Elijah Project*. Our little town rolled out the red carpet for the film crew of the movie titled *Catching Faith*. We opened our home, shared meals, gave everything—including a car a parishioner had donated, just so the crew could get around. It was amazing to experience moviemaking firsthand, and watching words we'd written come alive on screen was pure magic. Then the credits rolled, the crew flew home, and we were left financially broken and emotionally hollow.

> I had been living a dream in reverse.

By late August, Perry's pastor's salary, slashed by church cuts, couldn't keep us afloat. We were selling plasma for groceries and gas. I had been a stay-at-home mom for ten years, living the life I'd always dreamed of, raising three beautiful children. But as the weeks rolled into months, we became more desperate, and change became inevitable.

My husband also rejoined his profession of the past, working as an optician. Perry took a third job unloading iconic brown delivery trucks at 3:00 a.m. In September, our youngest started second grade, and I began the terrifying process of interviewing again, ten years out of the professional world, armed only with faith and a rusty resume. It was time for me to contribute financially to our family budget.

Job offers didn't come swiftly. Then, one day when I was sitting in my hairdresser's chair (she'd just had her own cameo in our movie), she asked how I was doing. Before I could answer, she said, "I know someone drowning in therapy clients." She named a nearby town and mental health clinic. "Want me to connect you?"

My stomach dropped, but I heard myself say, "Yes, please."

A week later, while celebrating my dad's seventy-fifth birthday in New England, I got the call: the job was mine. I could start when I got home.

Embracing Opportunity

This job was literally manna from heaven. I didn't even say yes to my friend before she suggested the job and agreed to put a good word in for me. For me, this wasn't throwing boxes at a package delivery warehouse—a menial task for my husband. It was actually a job in my profession with people who seemed to be like-minded and where I would have an opportunity to grow.

> This job was literally manna from heaven.

So, there I was on that arctic morning, engine blown, late for my first staff meeting, sitting in McDonald's, clutching coffee and fighting back tears. Losing the freedom to be the full-time mother that I'd been for a decade broke something sacred inside me. My youngest would get a different version of her mother than the older two had known, and that grief sat heavy all winter.

Yet something else was rising: a resilience I didn't know I possessed.

My boss, Donna, didn't fire me for missing day one. She gave me grace, and that job was flexible and meaningful. It was only a few days a week, so I could still be home when the bus rolled up. It ended up being a gift from God, one that I couldn't have masterminded or planned for. It was a sign of my heavenly Father's unmerited favor.

Re-entering the workforce at forty-two felt humiliating and exhilarating at the same time. While my colleagues had sharpened their skills, I had wiped noses, packed lunches, and cleaned crayon off walls. Thankfully, Donna saw something in me despite my lost time. Her hiring me changed the course of my life's trajectory.

That broken-down Chevy on the side of I-94 became a symbol: Sometimes the thing that falls apart is the very thing that forces you forward.

Forging a Way Through

This new life demanded grit and grace in equal measure. Perry rearranged his entire ministry around kids' schedules. Our middle school daughter learned to cook dinner twice a week with a meal-kit subscription. I had to let go of control, of perfection, of chores done "my way." Survival meant surrender, and surrender, miraculously, made room for a bigger life and a miraculously bigger version of me.

> Saying yes cracked the door to adventures I never could have scripted.

Saying yes—to the job, to help from strangers, to imperfect dinners, and a husband who vacuumed when I once would have—cracked the door to adventures I never could have scripted.

My time at that clinic gave me courage and eventually led

me to open my own small private practice. I wrote more books and screenplays. The job was flexible and allowed me to be on set for future film projects. While filming a Christmas movie at my parents' church in Massachusetts, I stumbled into a love for production design. Something else I would have never known if I hadn't said yes when the opportunity presented itself. My girls got a chance to act alongside a popular sitcom mom. This was a friendship I never would have dreamed of having. The Christmas movie also brought with it an opportunity to work with all three of my siblings at the same time, something that has not repeated itself to date. Those days of creativity brought joy and a shared once-in-a-lifetime memory.

We shot two movies in Kentucky, again with my daughters by my side. The journey led me to fly to Georgia on a red-eye to scout locations for another film after my daughter's curtain call in a starring role. On another occasion, I coached her through a theater crisis from a hotel room in Los Angeles. This was a new way of mothering, but it somehow worked.

The same muscle that once allowed me to survive sleepless nights and toddler tantrums now let me say yes when every part of me wanted to say no.

The resilience forged on that frozen highway, in that white Cadillac that stopped for a stranger and in the McDonald's booth, brought a renaissance of sorts for me. The hundred tiny surrenders ended up carrying me into rooms I never dared dream I would visit.

Life guarantees one thing: If you endure the hard moments when the intensity seems unmanageable, there is a promise of a new perspective on the other side. Sometimes the changes you are faced with break your heart. Sometimes it breaks you open. And sometimes, when a door flies open on the side of a frigid highway and a kind voice offers, "Let me help you stay warm," resilience whispers back: "Yes, you can."

When a Few Words Matter

JONI TOPPER

I ASKED MY WITTY HUSBAND WHAT event in our lives he thought displayed our ability to be resilient. His response, "All of it," made me laugh. I could tell by his tone that he was not kidding. He's given me a lot of good advice through the years. Some of which I found wise in the moment, and some of which made me mad until I stepped back to process what he said.

WHEN I WAS JUST TWENTY-NINE years old, we did not have cell phones. Then every phone caller was a mystery until you could identify the voice on the line. A series of events began that caused my husband, Ernest, to offer me some great advice.

My dad had a heart attack while he was training for his job. He lived in Odessa, but his course was in San Antonio. Those cities are about a six-hour drive from each other, but San Antonio is only an hour from where I live. The phone call that informed me about his emergency came from my sister. "I'm catching a bus in Odessa, and I need you to pick me up at the bus stop when I arrive in San Antonio. We can go to the hospital together to be with Dad."

I dropped everything and headed to the bus stop. Ernest stayed home with the kids. There were no maps other than paper ones in those days. Furthermore, I did not know my way around that city, making the search unsettling. My angst over Dad's health, compounded by the discomfort of driving in the big city and wandering through the huge Greyhound station, left me a wobbly mess.

When I finally found the place, with sweaty palms and an anxious stomach, I watched amid the mass of humanity that came and went from that dirty bus stop. Load after load of travelers came and went, and there was no sign of my sister. She had informed me when her bus would arrive. I knew I was at the correct drop point, but she was nowhere to be found. After an hour and a half, I opted to leave and go to the hospital. Sure enough; she was there. Her bus had arrived early, and she'd caught a cab.

I dropped my inclination to be angry with her for sending me to the creepy part of town because both of us needed to focus on Dad's situation. The truth is, she could not have reached me anyway because neither one of us had a phone. It's hard even to remember the times when communications were so delayed before cell phones. There were many situations that today's younger generation would have a hard time relating to because our instant, real-time information about everyone and everything has made us impatient with the concept of waiting.

> Something about having to wait teaches us to assess situations more accurately.

I believe this has also contributed to having a harder time being resilient. We are not accustomed to any unknown factors in our lives anymore. Something about having to wait teaches us to assess situations more accurately. It gives us time to think things through.

My dad lived through this episode with little damage to his heart and resumed his normal lifestyle soon thereafter. Then, a few months later, I got another one of those calls. This time it felt more serious, and I began to get a sick feeling in my stomach every time the phone rang. When I reached out to answer, my husband saw the distress on my face numerous times.

Words of Redirection

One night when the phone rang, Ernest stopped me after I hung up from talking with a friend. "Would you stop doing that?" he said.

His tone irritated me. It felt confrontational at that moment. "Stop what?" I asked.

"Stop panicking and feeling that dread every time you reach for the phone. One of these days, you will get a hard phone call about your dad. It will be plenty bad on that day. There is no reason to live it over and over again before it happens. Stop doing that to yourself." His words stung, yet they were rational. They were good advice.

My dad went on to have three more heart events after that over the next several years, but I stopped dreading every time the phone rang. Like so much other good advice people have given me through the years, the key to its effectiveness is what we *decide* about the advice. My acceptance of adopting a new attitude when circumstances were difficult would make the difference. The situations don't stop being hard when they happen, but he was correct; there's no benefit in living them over and over unnecessarily. My dad lived another twenty-six years. It was not his heart that caused his death after all.

Ernest's words have come to mind again more recently.

Unwelcome Words

Over the last four years, my husband has had four surgical heart procedures. His doctor has informed us that the last two did not solve his problem. On our last visit to the heart surgeon, he spelled out some new options for correcting the issue. We are weary of these ongoing surgeries. None of them should be life-threatening, and yet, with each new procedure, we are not oblivious to the reality that our lives could change in a literal heartbeat and never be the same again. I began having that sick feeling of dread again, and I remembered those words from long ago. "Don't do that to yourself."

When we left that last appointment with the surgeon, we drove for a while in silence. I could tell both of our minds were spinning. I looked at Ernest and said, "You know, the bright side of all of this is that even with the issues, you don't feel particularly bad, and life keeps on being pretty normal." We discussed our blessings in the middle of this trial.

> Each day is a beautiful opportunity.

In some ways, it does not even seem correct to call it a trial, but I think that's because we've chosen to trust God's sovereignty in the matter. We will take the actions that we know to take and carry on with our ministries, having a clear understanding that each day is a beautiful opportunity. My husband is seventy-four, and he has been a pastor at the same church for thirty years. He's not talking about retirement, and *we* are not dwelling on negative "what ifs."

Redefining Words

When there is a situation in life that taunts me toward that nasty trap of worrying, I'm trying to remember that I can reframe the situation. Awareness is not the same thing as worry. Awareness allows me to address situations from an active standpoint. For instance, my husband told me that we are going to take our goats to market and sell them next week.

"Why?" I asked.

"So when I have my surgery and can't lift anything for several weeks, you won't have to feed them every day, and I won't worry about the billy goat knocking you down when you go out there. We can buy more goats in the spring." His plan addressed our short-term and long-term needs in a way that reduces stress on both of us.

Wise words have a way of reappearing. My mom made us memorize Scripture when I was a teenager, and sometimes those verses come back to my mind in response to life events. I remember that Jesus addressed the emotion of worry.

> "That is why I tell you not to worry about everyday life—whether you have enough food and drink, or enough clothes to wear. Isn't life more than food, and your body more than clothing? Look at the birds. They don't plant or harvest or store food in barns, for your heavenly Father feeds them. And aren't you far more valuable to him than they are? Can all your worries add a single moment to your life?" (Matthew 6:25–27)

Part of the ability to live with resilience in the hard moments lies in the depth to which a situation pulls us down. Not giving in to the inclination to be paralyzed makes our ability to get moving again easier. Jesus knew this when he reminded us that worry won't change anything; it only weighs us down. Today, I'm thankful for those words from Scripture and also for those words from my husband, which have helped me choose a redo of my attitude. They made all the difference.

The Step After the Pause

BROOKE R. HACKMAN

AS A PARENT, UNCERTAINTY WEIGHS heavily when your child faces adversity—be it a school bully, unavoidable peer pressure, or self-imposed struggles fueled by perfectionism, expectations, or loss.

To date, my most difficult out-of-body experience with adversity relating to my child was when my four-year-old son was diagnosed with cancer. It was as if his body had betrayed both him and me, since it was part of my body that gave him form.

We were sitting in his pediatrician's office, waiting for routine bloodwork to be processed, when his doctor came in and asked me to go to our local children's hospital to "make sure my machine is working correctly," based on the readings she was just given. According to her, it was more out of curiosity than sudden alarm. I remember the day like it was yesterday (Saint Patrick's Day to be exact), when my husband and I traveled thirty minutes to a looming health facility that was only supposed to be a precautionary (and transient) step.

Fast forward three days later, and we found out our child did not have a virus. Leukemia was in full force at 70 percent in his little body, and chemotherapy was his best hope for survival. His cancer, acute myeloid leukemia (AML), was a ticket to a six-month minimum hospital admission and an unexpected bone marrow transplant when his first round of chemo did not work.

We went from celebrating his recent birthday and playing with bubbles outside to an implanted port and playdates down the hall of an oncology ward.

> I learned I was only as strong as the inherent traits I was forced to put into practice.

Of course, I was completely unprepared for it all. Yet there was a peace that surpassed my understanding that took hold. There was a grit, from both my husband and me, that decided we would not lose our faith in God. We would hold it together day in and day out, not just for our child, but for ourselves, because crumbling was simply not an option. I learned I was only as strong as the inherent traits I was forced to put into practice. In situations like these, joy is restored one good piece of information at a time.

Don't get me wrong, there were days of lament, terror, and anger. Especially when you stop and reflect on the cruel irony of how life is not fair, yet it is full of possibility. Even today, I tell all my children that fairness ended in the garden, but God's love and patience did not.

Spoiler alert: God healed my son. His healing wasn't simply due to modern medicine. On paper, that bone marrow transplant I mentioned earlier really shouldn't have been an option. My children are of mixed race, and such can make donor and recipient matching extremely difficult, if not improbable.

Cue God.

Our second son (who was one year old at the time) was evaluated as a possible match, along with my husband. To be a match, you must possess a certain number of genetic markers.

Wouldn't you know, my second child not only achieved that amount, but he surpassed it. Their original DNA is so close that it must be sent out to another lab to tell them apart. Pseudo twins, two years apart.

When people tell you to take life day by day, there is nothing better to describe *living* after a bone marrow transplant. Hour by hour, his young body was assessed to make sure his organs would accept one another and play nice with its new blood-based inhabitant.

Almost four months after admission, my son underwent a sibling-matched bone marrow donation. One month after that, we were discharged and put in charge of administering ten medications in as sterile an environment as our home could offer.

> God is a waymaker when his plan is still in motion and seemingly at a dead end.

That summer, we experienced multiple tube feeding interruptions, inexplicable fevers that required further hospital stays, and a new appreciation for grocery delivery so we were not exposed to public places. But we also experienced profound joy in waking up each morning in our home together, with the faith-fueled promise we were living within a new beginning and a clarity few are given access to. You only grow when the space you are in requires you to do so. There is no challenge in joy, only existence. As a caveman could explain, you don't need to learn to survive the Ice Age when the tree outside is full of fruit.

Perhaps this is a good place to mention how God is a waymaker when his plan is still in motion and seemingly at a dead end. I was adopted from India as an infant. Since I was eight years old, I knew God wanted me to fulfill the call of adoption for another little girl from the same country. Prior to our cancer journey, we had begun the process of adopting, but everything was immediately halted to care for our son. About four months after our son was discharged, my husband asked me if I was ready to restart the process.

I shared that I was uncertain about doing so, since it seemed the interruption of our son's illness was "surely" a sign that my dream was indeed just that, and not a destiny. He quickly reminded me that the two were in no way related, and because God had opened his heart to adoption as well, we were not going to allow the Enemy to steal what we were called to do and complete.

Cue God part two.

Our adopted daughter was born two years almost to the date our son was diagnosed with cancer. When I found out that stark coincidence, I felt God say, "Daughter, *this* (birthdate) is the day you must remember. I have replaced one day for another, and it is 'the joy that has come in the morning.'"

Sometimes reality puts us all in a place to realign our thinking and prove character. Dare I say, if you never find yourself in such situations, you might be squelching your days and wasting your potential.

> The wilderness of life is not just a place to survive. It is a place of holy education.

The wilderness of life is not just a place to survive. It is a place of holy education.

By the way, it is not lost to me the number of parents and people who travel through life a loved one fewer than they would choose. The death of anyone is a stark jolt of reality, and it seems that while some may not be as heavily weighted as others, some hit hard. Those with whom you've had an intimate relationship or with whom you've shared sacred moments just seem to ache deeper than maybe you even have words for.

For those of reeling from loss, it can take a substantial amount of time to understand that death teaches us that life cannot really be valued unless bereavement is experienced, and it creates an empathy you cannot replace. One of my favorite Bible teachers said that only those who have truly suffered can truly comfort.

> While in my wilderness season, it was difficult not to get stuck in the mindset that sorrow was my lot in life.

While in my wilderness season, it was difficult not to get stuck in the mindset that sorrow was my lot in life. I was required to seek out stories of triumph within my category of struggle, so I connected with parents whose children, at one point, received a similar diagnosis as my son but were blessed to be on the other side of cancer and bone marrow transplant. Their positivity and experiences served as a lifeline and a break in the clouds for me, even when the outlook was as gray as could be.

I also sought out Bible verses that struck a nerve and revealed the true meaning of what God says about his Word: that it is alive, active, on purpose, and discerning. For me, my verses are Jeremiah 29:11 and Genesis 15:5.

Jeremiah, because I know his ultimate plans past the garden are toward a promising future and *hope* (which also happens to be the middle name of my adopted daughter), not evil.

Genesis, because Abraham was divinely promised that his ancestors would outnumber the stars in the sky. As an orphan, it is difficult to imagine such, simply because you are always number one on your own family tree. But when my son was in treatment, I knew his medically induced pause was in no way a period. It was a comma that would lead to the type of story that our innumerable descendants would cling to, be proud of, and find purpose in. This verse also includes children who are adopted (legally or not), like my daughter, who find their way into a family and become tree branches (or stars) no matter their biological beginnings.

> After living through life's valleys and mountaintops, I understand that resiliency is certainly a decision and a step someone must take.

Merriam-Webster defines resilience as "an ability to recover from or adjust to misfortune or change."* After living through life's valleys and mountaintops, I understand that resiliency is certainly a decision and a step someone must take. In this forward movement, there is a sense of appreciation (elusive at times for sure) for all the things life still has to offer, no matter the adversity in motion during the time of my trials.

---

* *Merriam-Webster's Unabridged Dictionary*, s.v. "resilience," accessed December 30, 2025, https://unabridged.merriam-webster.com/unabridged/resilience.

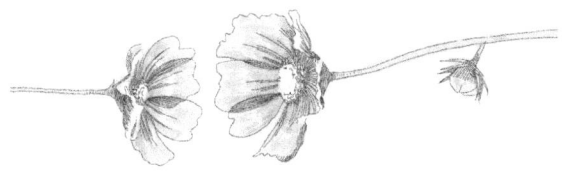

I Didn't Sign Up for This

LORI VOBER

LIFE IS FULL OF UNMET expectations, unplanned challenges, broken dreams, and altered journeys. Rarely do our paths turn out exactly like we dream about or expect them to. Not one of us is so bored with our lives that we raise our hand to sign up for the next life-altering challenge. But when life takes us through the storms we never saw coming, we realize that our dependence on God builds resilience and perseverance that could only come through his strength and the trust we learn to rely on through the twists and turns of our unplanned journeys.

At the younger age of twenty-nine, I desired to use my corporate marketing and sales skills in a more purpose-filled position and to settle down and become a mom. Three weeks into a new job as the office manager at our church and just shy of our fifth wedding anniversary, I suffered a life-changing intracerebral hemorrhagic stroke. My life and the lives of my family members were changed in the blink of an eye. I had no idea that I was a walking time bomb for such a medical disaster, but I was born with a malformation of blood vessels on the right side of my brain that was never diagnosed. When the malformation ruptured, it caused a massive brain bleed. Within an hour of stroke symptoms escalating and the paramedics being called to the church, I was unconscious and fighting for my life. I underwent emergency brain surgery to stop the brain bleed and woke up seventeen days later from a drug-induced coma, paralyzed on the left side.

Statistically, in 2003, when my stroke occurred, only 50 to 60 percent survived this type of stroke, my doctors had said. Of those that did survive, only 20 percent continued to live an independent life six months post-stroke. Those are sobering statistics for a twenty-nine-year-old and her family, but by the grace of God, I did survive. I went from complete independence to complete dependence. I couldn't even roll over on my own after my stroke, and all sense of modesty simply vanished.

After two months in the hospital and two brain surgeries, I was not given much hope of regaining additional function past six months of recovery. I left the hospital in a wheelchair. At that point, I could stand and walk short distances with assistance and with a four-pronged cane, and I had no movement in my left arm and hand.

> God had not only allowed me to survive this massive stroke, but he was completely rewriting my story.

I didn't realize it at the time, but God had not only allowed me to survive this massive stroke, but he was completely rewriting my story. Every stroke survivor and individual who fights through a medical challenge has a different recovery journey, and I believe God has a purpose and a plan for every trial we walk through. Because of my husband's job loss right after my stroke, due to the downturn of the aviation industry, we moved to Arizona from Minnesota six months post-stroke. In Arizona, I found a wonderful neuro rehab clinic that provided great new hope for my recovery and a path toward more independence. This clinic believed that recovery was possible with repetition to retrain the brain and hard work. For years, I made physical therapy my full-time job and was determined to be as mobile and independent as I possibly could be. I believe God gifted me the strength, drive, and resilience to positively persevere forward every day.

Stroke recovery is a lifelong journey, and after almost twenty-three years, I continue to work on my mobility and independence still today. Over the years, I thankfully have continued to make improvements, but the medical challenges have also continued. I developed epilepsy from the stroke soon after our move to Arizona, and it took years to find the right medicine to manage my seizures. As I published my first book in March 2022, I was pre-diagnosed with ovarian cancer and discovered during my hysterectomy surgery that I was unable to have children biologically, and I had been born with only one kidney.

> We want to trust God, but we also want a clear roadmap with all the details laid out.

We all go through unexpected trials, and many times, the course with our medical challenges is as clear as mud. We want to trust God, but we also want a clear roadmap with all the details laid out. As we continue to gain our strength to persevere through our trust in him, God not only is protecting us but is building new godly character traits within us. Many times, when we reflect, we discover God's intentions for us were so much greater than what we originally thought our journey was about.

Eight years post-stroke, God allowed my husband and me the desire of our hearts to be parents through international adoption.

We adopted a sibling group of three older children and felt called to provide a loving family to children who may never have that opportunity. Like all journeys, there were many unplanned challenges and learning opportunities. Had everything in our parenting journey turned out just like we expected, our dependence and trust in God and his plan would not have been the same. As humans, I believe it is all right that we have the emotions of frustration, sadness, grief, and even anger. But our strength and ability to persevere come from knowing that God is in control, he knows more than we know, and even when we don't understand the details of our crazy journey, we are safe in the palm of his hand. Philippians 4:6–7 reminds us that the peace we have by putting our hope and trust in God surpasses all human understanding.

Although I have a left side physical disability still today, God has guided me to an amazing new journey, and over time, I have learned to thrive in my new normal. My disability provides unique challenges at times, and I have had to learn that my body's ability and my heart aren't always going to be in sync. My disability is also a special part of my testimony, and I have learned to appreciate it, like a special God-purpose-filled gift.

> I have learned to appreciate it, like a special God-purpose-filled gift.

Without my journey of ongoing medical challenges and the experiences we learned through tough adoptive parenting, I know I would not have the same dependence on God and understanding of what hope and true joy look like, which is much different from the emotion of happiness that the world depends on. Sometimes, it is easier to run life's race with confidence when you can see the goal at hand and understand clearly the steps to take to reach that goal.

With medical challenges, many times the details aren't clear. Our resilience comes from our faith and blind trust in God's plans. We stop seeing things as our plans versus God's plans, and it becomes our desires on his journey. Had all my challenges not occurred, my perspective and faith would not be the same as they are today.

> We stop seeing things as our plans versus God's plans, and it becomes our desires on his journey.

If we stay in our lanes and only say yes to the things we feel comfortable with, we leave no room for God to teach us, grow us, and help us build the resilience he desires for us to have. I have learned through my experiences that when we go down the path we wouldn't typically choose for ourselves—sometimes kicking and screaming—God is still in control, protecting, supporting, and loving us each step of the way. God just wants us to fasten our seatbelts, stop asking questions, and trust him.

When we do that, he can take us on an unbelievable ride, where his plans are far greater than our plans. Proverbs 3:5–6 says, "Trust in the Lord with all your heart; do not depend on your own understanding. Seek his will in all you do, and he will show you which path to take."

In addition to physical recovery, God has taken me on an amazing journey of learning who I am through his eyes. No matter who we are, what our challenges are, or what we struggle with, our identity, security, and purpose can be difficult for each of us. As I have struggled to keep up with my peers, fit in with others, and find my place, God has met me in my places of grief, loneliness, and sorrow, and taught me some of the most important lessons that I would never have learned without struggling with a disability. We all have similar feelings of fitting in, but our identity must come from who

God calls us to be and says we are. Our desire to please him must become our central focus.

God takes what we see as broken pieces and puts them together, like brickwork on a path down his journey. Had my life gone as I had originally planned and desired, I might still be working at my church in Minnesota. I'd imagined two children, two dogs, and a calm life. That isn't my story. Through tragic events, miraculous recoveries, and an amazing relationship with the God who created me and never left my side, he has given me a life full of chaos, purpose, wonder, and understanding of hope and true joy.

Today, I am blessed to be an adoptive mom of three, a grandmother, a published author, and a motivational speaker. I am passionate about encouraging other stroke survivors and individuals facing unplanned medical challenges to find their trust and strength in God and be reminded that their purpose, like mine, often develops from the challenges they didn't raise their hand for as they rely on God for their strength and resilience to keep persevering forward.

For Such a Time

MAUREEN MILLER

THE THOUGHT PRODDED—*You need to start over.*

What? Was he kidding? So, I asked him, "God, do you mean it? Start over? Really?" But the silence was telling, and I knew. This was from God, and he was serious.

Weeks earlier, I'd hit send on my 100,000-word document, then waited. What I quickly learned was that many people who'd desired to write a book did so during this Isolation Age. My manuscript would, therefore, have to wait its turn.

This was June, near the beginning of the COVID-19 pandemic. When I flipped my desk calendar to the new month, with summer now in full force—though most were still fully masked—I couldn't help but wonder. When would I hear from my content editor? Where were my edits—those chunks of chapters needing tweaked to make my story shine?

Mind you, this was my first novel, and I knew I was far from being a perfect writer. Naturally, I'd expected to have an abundance of work ahead of me. I looked forward to getting busy, cutting and polishing so that my precious story might improve.

By mid-July, however, I was still waiting, and that's when the uncomfortable niggling began—insecurity, fear, dread. I was certain all my hard work was for nothing. Those five words that made me want to cry—*You need to start over*—caused me to question my gift as a writer. Honestly, I just didn't think I could do it.

And on one particularly difficult day, I proclaimed aloud to my reflection, "I'm giving up."

A Bit of Backstory

In 2007, I awoke on a bright spring morning with a phrase ringing in my mind: *The Bible by the bed.*

I thought it was God, but I wanted to be sure. "What?" I inquired.

It came again. *The Bible by the bed.* Familiar with his voice, I knew it was a commission of some sort. But for what?

It's difficult to explain all the ways God confirmed he had a plan, but I believed in my heart there was a story he wanted me to write. What I knew: it had something to do with a Gideon Bible discovered in a hotel room's bedside table.* Within the Bible's pages were clues indicating someone had cracked its cover prior, introducing a mystery. But who had been there, and what clues did she leave? For what purpose?

> Truthfully, this whole line of questioning was a figurative thump to my noggin.

---

* A "Gideon Bible" refers to one distributed by The Gideons International, whose mission includes "distributing copies of God's Word in hotels, hospitals, shelters, and other places where people often seek hope," https://gideons.org/about.

Truthfully, this whole line of questioning was a figurative thump to my noggin. After all, this was fiction—as in a full-length novel—but there was one problem. I didn't write fiction.

Although I'd been writing for some time, my comfort zone was nonfiction—primarily articles and devotions. Still, I sensed God was calling me from my comfort, asking me instead to step into the uncharted waters of protagonists and antagonists, setting and plot, story arc and climax. *Sigh*.

I argued with God for a spell, trying to convince him he'd picked the wrong writer. But over time, a little spark of possibility grew into a flame—a passion that fueled a deep-seated (though yet unearthed) desire to give this new genre a try.

> I argued with God for a spell, trying to convince him he'd picked the wrong writer.

It wasn't the first time I'd considered writing fictitious stories. I was even quoted in our high school's newspaper my senior year, answering a question concerning post-graduation hopes and dreams with, "I want to write children's picture books one day."

"But God, this seems way different from a carefully crafted fairytale. Longer too. Are you sure I'm the one for this job?"

And again, he confirmed in a variety of ways, even using providentially placed Gideon Bibles from time to time.

Armed with God's affirmation, I attended a Christian writers' conference in 2007. The keynote speaker—a man who's not only a prolific writer but an encourager-extraordinaire—spoke to my heart. In several of his sessions, he repeated the phrase over and over, "Hone your craft."

Because I intended to return home from this weekend-long conference and pursue the craft of fiction writing, I chose related workshops while there. I even rallied enough courage to sign up for a one-on-one with a representative from a large traditional publishing house. With only a few lines on paper, I offered her a copy of my one-page and shared the story on my heart.

"I love it," she exclaimed, then continued, "When you've finished your first draft, send me the first chapter in an envelope, indicating the conference name and year. I'll take a look."

Was she kidding? I didn't have to query or write a proposal? Just send her the first chapter of my finished manuscript? This seemed too good to be true, though these sorts of "open doors" are one of the many benefits for those attending conferences of this nature.

The fire inside burned more intensely, and I returned home to North Carolina ready to get to work. But . . .

Not long after, we lost a daughter to a failed adoption—learning after almost a year with her that her biological grandmother would be adopting her instead.

Soon after, my husband was diagnosed with a rare autoimmune disease requiring several surgeries and months of medications, causing their own complications.

> I fell into a pit of despair for a season—angry with the woman who "stole" our daughter. Angry at God for allowing the pain and suffering of my husband.

And me? I fell into a pit of despair for a season—angry with the woman who "stole" our daughter. Angry at God for allowing the pain and suffering of my husband. Angry at myself for . . . being angry.

Needless to say, my book didn't get written, though it remained an ember in my heart for years. I did continue to write within my comfort zone—nonfiction essays, articles, and devotions. I figured

I could at least hone my craft in this manner during this difficult season. And God in his mercy often reminded me, using words from Esther 4:14, "For such a time."

Fast Forward

Finally, in 2018, I began to write the story I'd titled *The Bible by the Bed*. Then, in June 2019, I attended that same writers' conference again, this time with a more professional one-page. After praying for wisdom, I sat down with a representative from a hybrid publishing house to share my story idea, which she loved.

I returned home eager to continue what I'd started, and I signed a contract with this publisher later that same year. My hope was to finish my first draft in early 2020.

Of course, we all know what happened early that year, but COVID didn't stop me. In fact, with our eleven-year-old daughter attending school online, I was able to work more from home. Though several months off my intended target, I hit send on my work in progress in early June, with hopes to get edits back quickly and finish what, by this time, had taken more than a dozen years to complete.

Hone Your Craft

As mentioned, I waited. And waited. And yes, I grew frustrated. That particular morning when I'd looked myself in the eye in our bathroom mirror and proclaimed, "I'm giving up," was actually a moment of reckoning. It was then I realized the meaning of the great western writer Louis L'Amour's words, "There will come a time when you believe everything is finished. That will be the beginning."[*]

And I heard God again—*You need to start over.*

---

[*] Louis L'Amour, *Lonely on the Mountain* (New York: Bantam Books, 1980), 1.

Only this time, I kept myself from arguing. Instead, I surrendered the story I knew was God's first, believing it was him who'd birthed the idea in my heart all those years ago, for a greater purpose.

If I was going to start over, then I truly needed, as I'd been encouraged in 2007, to *hone my craft*. Because, truth was, I really didn't know how to write quality fiction—not for children's picture books, not for a full-length novel.

So, I got busy reading quality fiction. I read about writing quality fiction. I listened to podcasts teaching on the craft of quality fiction. And guess what. In time, I learned better how to write quality fiction.

> It didn't happen overnight. It took time. And sometimes, many times, I took breaks.

It didn't happen overnight. It took time. And sometimes, many times, I took breaks. During these sabbaticals, I continued to hone my craft of nonfiction writing, finding ways to write collaboratively—what I call "teamwork writing." I discovered I loved writing with others, sharing devotions, essays, and articles under umbrella "anthology" themes as diverse as one can imagine—from dogs to divine moments, from stories of heartbreak to ones of humor.

The Birth of a Novel

Four years after sending my first draft, I hit send again on the story God whispered to my heart so many years earlier.

And I heard him once more, though on this occasion God

finished what he'd started, using that same Esther passage—"For such a time . . ."—only this time, he added, "as this."

It was as if I heard him say, *Maureen, you thought you knew right when this story should be in the world, but my thoughts—my ways—are much higher. My words never return void but accomplish that which I purpose. Through this experience, you've learned so much more than simply about becoming a better writer. You've learned to trust me, even when it was difficult. Even when you were frustrated. Even when you wanted to give up. But can you see? This story—it's for now.*

And it's true. With its new title, *Gideon's Book*—despite its author being far from perfect, with so much room to grow—was born in the world at an appointed time, for God's intended purpose.

I can't help but personalize this now favorite passage, believing it was God who spoke these words to my heart, to encourage me to stay the course: "If you keep quiet at a time like this, deliverance and relief . . . will arise from some other place . . . Who knows if perhaps you were made [a fiction writer] for just such a time as this?" (Esther 4:14).

Oh, and may it be so.

Words Enough for Today

HEATHER VOGLER

WHY WAS THE ROOM SPINNING? I tried to get my bearings. The unmade bed, which my two-year-old daughter and I had used for story time that morning, began to fade. The pink plush blanket comforted my crisscrossed legs as my field of vision gradually disappeared.

Maybe I should lie down. The thought slowly passed through my mind like a tornado warning on the bottom of a newscast—alerting you, but not the main focus of the show.

I'm fine, I concluded as I stood up, determined to face the day regardless of how I felt. *I handled the discomforts of pregnancy in the past; I can handle this minor inconvenience now.*

Bam!

I found myself flat on the floor in seconds. Maybe I pushed myself too hard. Maybe I was too stubborn. I was not on the floor long when the morning sun, spilling through an eastern window of our home, forced me to squint.

Good, I am conscious, my mind reasoned. *I did not pass out.*

As I opened my mouth to assure my four- and five-year-old sons that Mommy was fine, nothing came out. Not a word. My mind was carefully crafting what I wanted to convey, like a well-thought-out social media post, but the words were stuck in my brain—they would not come out. After what felt longer than a wait at the DMV, I could speak, but not what I intended to say. The words were complete gibberish.

Trying to Stay Calm for the Kids

I attempted to speak coherently, but what were these nonsensical words exiting my lips? My mind was sharper than the recently honed tools in my husband's shop, but nothing was cutting through. I was unable to communicate to my kids the recurring message that they needed to hear: "Go get me the phone!"

> I attempted to speak coherently, but what were these nonsensical words exiting my lips?

Would that really help, though? They are too young to call their dad, I thought.

We only had a landline, and I wasn't savvy enough to put his work number on speed dial for emergencies like this. And it certainly didn't seem like a 9-1-1 emergency—yet.

Sprawled out on the well-worn but cozy primary-colored accent rug in the middle of the room, I rested there for what seemed like hours but must have been only a few minutes since the three little ones did not burn the house down. They bounced from room to room, as if it were an ordinary weekday morning, carrying noisy, battery-powered toys from one end of the house to the other. I kept trying to speak to them, only to hear strange words.

I finally figured out that if I only tried to say one word at a time, I could, for a little while at least, before it tired me out. Finally, all

I had to say was, "Phone," while pointing to the other room. My oldest son got the picture.

An Understanding Husband

Now came the intimidating part. Calling the office of my husband's work. My heart beat hard against my chest as I realized that the secretary would not know how to respond. I slowly said each word, praying the whole time. She quickly found my husband, and he rushed home.

As soon as he realized that I could not speak, he handed me a pen and paper. Fear paralyzed me as I realized that my hand wouldn't write either. I attempted to tell him everything. The scribbles said it all.

What happened next was pivotal. My husband brought me to the bed and told me to rest, but I was not tired. I lay there thinking about what my life would be like if I could not do what I felt called to do for the Lord anymore. I wanted to speak life to others. To encourage them. That was my first thought that came to mind as I lay there. I couldn't help but cry.

As the tears flowed, I was reminded of different young ladies I knew who'd had a brain injury and could no longer speak. A vibrant classmate from high school was injured by a drunk driver and can only communicate by blinking. An ambitious, mission-minded young lady from church now has brain cancer, confining her to a wheelchair and leaving her unable to speak well.

> I prayed desperately that I didn't have permanent damage.

I prayed desperately that I didn't have permanent damage, but if I did, I realized that even though it wasn't in the same way as before,

God was still using them now, and he could use me too—regardless.

Not a Stroke, Not a Clue

The day ended in a visit to the ER with inconclusive findings. An MRI revealed it was not a stroke. Ten years of doctor visits, tests, and scans have showed nothing. The stuttering was sporadic, but intelligible. When it would happen, my friends would laugh it off, and I would too, even though inside I was screaming, "Can't you see something is wrong with me, here! Please help me!" I had never stuttered before that day.

That first year, I was unable to drive. My brain simply would not let me. The first time I tried, I was halfway down the street and had to pull over due to confusion. *Where am I? What town am I in? What is going on?* In my mid-thirties, this seemed unusual, but our family made it work. Once an independent world traveler, now completely dependent on my husband to leave the house, I learned a tremendous deal about myself that year and in the years to come.

> I learned a tremendous deal about myself that year and in the years to come.

I also learned who my true friends were. My life changed dramatically since I couldn't cart my kids to birthday parties and playdates anymore; we were able to focus on family time and each other. Since they were home more than I had anticipated, they learned to cook, garden, and work on handicrafts at a young age. We read more books than you can dream of. As the years went on, they learned to help around the house and have patience when Mom needed a few hours before she could easily form a sentence. Charades was a normal way of communicating.

When Life Gives You Lemons

The light at the end of the tunnel gave me a glimmer of hope that God had a plan in all of this when I saw that God was using my experiences to help others. A friend unexpectedly had a brain aneurysm and could barely speak. His family ensured that he received the best care from the country's top doctors. Still, his speech was limited. When we visited him, I was able to show compassion in a way that I had never imagined. Although he was unable to communicate well, I shared that I understood how hard it was to have once been so vibrant and full of life and, in an instant, feel trapped.

> The compassion that my kids developed through this experience helped me persevere.

I could tell he understood as I spoke. My sons, full of compassion because of what they had experienced at home with me over the years, prayed for him, right there in the hospital. Faintly, he thanked them verbally. We all heard it, even though he hadn't spoken for the three days prior. The compassion that my kids developed through this experience helped me persevere.

I kept seeking ways to heal, and after ten years, it happened in a way that changed the course of my life suddenly. In a way that only God can orchestrate. Within a twenty-four-hour period, I spoke to three women, in different conversations, who all had the same symptoms that I did. This led me to seek a different form of testing, which came back positive for Lyme disease and other co-infections. I'd had it so long that it had gone into my bloodstream and affected my brain. I found natural treatments that have helped me keep the symptoms under control and live a normal life.

A few years later—in a room that had standing room only at a state homeschool convention—once the butterflies subsided, I found myself speaking to new homeschool moms about how to teach their children, how to make it through the tough days, weeks, or even months. The God who knows the number of hairs on my head, the one who gave me the resilience to walk through days doing what I was called to do, even when I felt inadequate, gave me the strength I needed.

> I saw that he was made strong in my weakness as I was able to encourage—to speak life.

That day was the dawn of a new beginning. I saw that he was made strong in my weakness as I was able to encourage—to speak life. Only by the grace of God, I continue to do so to this day.

Courage

The Step That Changed Everything

TASHA SCHUH

I DON'T ACTUALLY KNOW WHEN I learned the meaning of the word *resilience*. Long after I started living it—being it—out of necessity after my accident, the accident that left me a C5 quadriplegic with a broken neck and a severely crushed spinal cord. The accident that ended my dreams of ever again running the length of a basketball court on two healthy legs or riding my bike on a rustic road with friends. The accident that stole my hopes of pursuing musical theater in college, with a vision of starring on Broadway someday. In truth, the accident probably proved that I already possessed some qualities of resilience, although life had been pretty easy up to that point.

But what kid thinks her life is easy? I believed I was being challenged. I had all the usual struggles. Like the struggle to be a starter in volleyball, or the struggle to find the confidence to audition for my school's musical. Yet, the accident taught me the real definition of resilience and what it would take to restart my life—if I were fortunate enough to survive.

At the age of sixteen, just days before my high school opened its production of *The Wizard of Oz*, I took one step backward during a rehearsal and fell sixteen feet through a stage trap door that had just been opened for the upcoming scene. On that day, November 11, 1997, my life changed forever. That sixteen-foot drop landed me on the concrete basement floor of the Sheldon Theater, an ornate historic building in Red Wing, Minnesota, where my Western Wisconsin high school completed its run of *The Wizard of Oz* without me.

> I took one step backward during a rehearsal and fell sixteen feet through a stage trap door.

With friends, music teachers, and the director watching, Red Wing paramedics transported me out, heading to the local hospital, only to learn that a Life Link helicopter had been ordered. The ICU at the major medical complex in Rochester was about a twenty-minute airlift away.

On that transport, I vomited up my donut and hot chocolate that I had consumed just prior to play practice. This would haunt me later, as the lung aspiration became another threat to my life. Weeks of intubation took my voice away, although staff and family members helped me learn a slow system of communication with my eyes. I spelled out words and sentences, one letter at a time, as I focused on the alphabet board. Visitors and round-the-clock staff cheered me on, although everyone still questioned my ability to survive.

A major surgery to salvage a slim chance of mobility led to post-op complications, which nearly took my life. Septic shock, they called it. My peak body temperature of 108 degrees led the doctors to level with my family. "Spend time with her now. She will not likely survive tonight."

My family told me later that my coma lasted for eight days with that spiked body temp and extremely low blood pressure. At one point, a Code Blue call was announced, my team of ICU experts overflowed the room, and my family was told they needed to say goodbye. An exhausting process of manually maintaining life support lasted for hours. Family and staff shouted to no response, "Tasha, come on. You can do this! You've got to hang on. Fight!"

I can still recall my frightening coma dreams, yet I never heard the crowded room begging me to fight and wake up. After the drama of this eight-day setback, the new Tasha Schuh finally opened her eyes.

The good news: I was conscious.

The bad news: my neck was broken; pieces of it severely crushed my spinal cord.

> The good news: I was conscious.
> The bad news: my neck was broken; pieces of it severely crushed my spinal cord.

It was here that the doctors told me I would never walk again. Devastation does not begin to describe how I felt from hearing those words. Dark thoughts kept asking, *Why hadn't I just died?*

As I began my rehabilitation, I realized that I had so much learning to do. And before I could learn the many skills needed to navigate life from a wheelchair, my body had to heal. I would spend five months in total at Rochester, my mom abandoning her post at home and work to live in the Ronald McDonald House two blocks away from the medical campus. Just being near me, to support me, mattered so much. I battled anxiety and depression as I worked to accept my life in what felt like a stranger's uncooperative body.

I won't lie; it was dark. Days were difficult. But when I confronted the reality with tears and denial, nothing changed. I had to change. I had to shift my mindset, although no one called it that back then. I had to decide I would participate. I had to heal and learn new ways to see myself in the world. I had to listen to the medical experts—like my physical and occupational therapists—people who could teach me to maximize whatever mobility I could muster.

> I was excited about the possibility of college and wanted to prove any naysayers wrong.

With support and what felt like tough love, I graduated from high school on schedule with my class. Resilience wasn't really the word used then. Yet, I was making progress. I was excited about the possibility of college and wanted to prove any naysayers wrong. Of course, this was long before coursework could be found online. In fact, very few college campuses were ADA-compliant (Americans with Disabilities Act). My family never doubted my desire to attend a university.

So, I researched and found that Winona State University seemed most willing to help me overcome the new obstacles I faced. I would need an accessible dorm room, daily assistance from caregivers, and other accommodations, such as note-taking assistance. I was willing to find and train the people who could help keep my college dream alive. Yet, I knew my journey from surviving to thriving would not be easy.

I had grown up going to church, yet I admittedly did not have a strong faith at this point. A new, difficult second chance at life for me meant leaving my dreams behind and starting over. I was mad at God. Yet, an experience at a local church turned the tide for me.

A few years after my accident—I will not forget this turning point—I had a leap of faith. A guest speaker broke a barrier for me. This man's story did not resemble mine in any way except that he, too, had struggled with faith. He had to experience bad things before he saw the truth. His message resonated strongly with me. *Had God sent this speaker to me directly?*

> I had been granted a second chance.

I finally acknowledged the truth: I had been granted a second chance. Rather than being angry with God, I was seeing that I could trust him. As I began to see his goodness and faithfulness in my life, I asked him to use my life to help and inspire others who experienced their own struggles. This was probably the most important step in my resilience journey—learning to be grateful for life and learning to ask God for help with every new corner I turned.

My devastating accident completely changed the trajectory of my life. What I thought was over, or utterly hopeless, became a life far better than I had ever imagined before my accident. Through resilience and strong support from my family—and in recent years, my husband, Doug—I learned that giving up is never an option. For example, I didn't just want a college degree; I pushed for top grades. I graduated from Winona State University, majoring in communication studies, with a minor in music. (One of my doctors broke the news to me that I would never sing again. My music minor proved him wrong. Now I share this fact with audiences and close every presentation with a song.) Because of my focus on faith, I immediately pursued a second college degree in theology and graduated with a 4.0 GPA.

At times, some of my accomplishments surprise people. For example, early on in my new life, I learned how to drive a minivan, despite the minimal use of my arms. With my dad's courage as driving partner and a very expensive adaptive conversion, I earned my driver's license for the second time in my young life. I can tell you I was grateful for it when I found the courage to meet Doug at a coffee shop for our first date, many miles from my home. (Nervous to meet Doug, I left the house late. I thank the Lord I did not get a speeding ticket on I-94 that day.)

> I designed my own home and began living independently with some help from caregivers.

Not long after college, I designed my own home and began living independently with some help from caregivers. I have people start and end my days—about four hours per day, usually working in teams of two. This is definitely less support than my doctors originally thought I would require. Yet, a big part of my day depends on reliable caregivers. I recruit, hire, and serve as both client *and* employer still to this day.

In 2007, I began speaking full-time, using my story to inspire others to build resilience and maintain positive mental health when facing life's unexpected challenges. This speaking career started with some home-printed brochures and old-fashioned word-of-mouth support from people who knew my story. Those brochures started me on a speaking career that hasn't slowed down.

In 2012, I was crowned Miss Wheelchair USA, and the following year, in August 2013, I became happily married to my Prince Charming, Doug. I was honored to represent Mayo Clinic after they nominated me, and I was chosen as the recipient of the National Rehabilitation Champion Award (2012). In 2014, I received the Distinguished Young Alumni Award from my alma mater, Winona State University. Soon after, I was honored to receive the Falconer Award (2016), which was meaningful since it came from our Wisconsin State Governor's Committee for People with Disabilities.

I have written and published two memoirs about my journey. And in 2025, I was inducted into the inaugural Ellsworth Community School District Hall of Fame.

Today, I speak in schools, organizations, and to professionals across the country. My Power of PATH message, which defines the acronym Purpose, Attitude, Team, and Hope, is intended for both youth and adults. PATH represents the four tools that helped me recover and learn how to thrive after my accident. The Power of PATH transfers to any level of adversity, equipping people with skills to build resilience, just as I have in my life. For elementary students, my husband Doug and I present the Build Your Brave message, sharing the importance of resilience and kindness, the power of a positive attitude, and how to overcome fears.

Most recently, I have become a resilience coach, helping people face life's greatest adversities, building resilience and joy, while using the tools I've gained from over thirty years of living as a quadriplegic.

> Adversity is a part of the human condition. And resilience is not an easy road.

Adversity is a part of the human condition. And resilience is not an easy road. But finding the motivation and courage it takes to improve our circumstances is a valuable way to move forward. The work it takes to see the good around us is so worth it. When we open our eyes to what feels meaningful, what is within our ability to control or change, we apply the skills of resilience. When we ask for support from caring, capable people who, by the way, will also gain from sharing their talents and abilities, we can continue to seek and find the hope for a life that includes happier days.

Because of my accident, I found my mission in life. Inspiring others to face their own "trap doors" has given my life a strong sense of purpose. Life is challenging; life throws unexpected curveballs at us. Resilience is the ability to defy the odds. It isn't easy, but the rewards are sweet. Resilience didn't just help me rise; it helped me create a life I truly love.

Different Doesn't Mean Disordered

LISA L. CROWE

I WAS TERRIFIED. I WAS FIFTY-TWO years old and three years away from retirement. And once again, I was on an improvement plan at work. I loved parts of my job as a case manager for families who had children with disabilities. I enjoyed visiting them in their homes and was an avid researcher. If a child had a rare condition, I would learn as much as I could about it so I could make the right connections for the family. But I wasn't a good organizer. I pushed the limits with deadlines. And I missed important details.

I had been in that role for about eight years. While I had thrived at first, I was increasingly stifled by the regulations and deadlines common in public sector jobs. My performance review scores had plummeted. And it seemed as if I would fix one issue, only to be bombarded by another deficiency.

We answered to both federal and state authorities and had to navigate an increasingly tangled web of regulations. Some of my coworkers had no difficulty with the complicated process. Many of us struggled. But none worse than me.

My superiors were also frustrated. And I was concerned they were building a case to terminate me, not a pleasant prospect for anyone. But I had spent my entire career in state service, and I had no idea how I would find another job if I lost this one.

I closed myself in my office so no one would see the tears welling in my eyes and read over the paperwork that detailed my latest failures in the eyes of my bosses. I hadn't missed any deadlines, but they insisted I wasn't monitoring various markers closely enough, and a failure on my part could impact the entire agency.

"Great," I mumbled. "More monitoring. More spreadsheets. More chances to fail." I had no idea how I would ever get out of the mess.

Then I noticed something I hadn't noticed before. In a box above the signature line that informed me of my rights, there was a phone number to the state's Employee Assistance Plan network. It's a contract program that helps employees with a variety of issues that interfere with work. I knew about it but had never consulted it because I suspected it wasn't as private as it claimed to be.

> I had finally reached out for help and was shunted to voicemail.

But at this point, I was desperate and didn't see that it could cause me any more problems. I called the number and got voicemail. That seemed like the ultimate insult. I had finally reached out for help and was shunted to voicemail. But I left my name and cell number, figuring that I might as well see this to the end.

I did get a call back. And they referred me to a local counselor. When I went in to see her, I was surprised by her line of questioning. She didn't focus only on the immediate issue but talked to me about how I managed in middle school, high school, and other jobs.

A pattern began to emerge. I had been a good student. But I was disorganized, often lost things, and had to redo assignments. I wrote papers at the last minute. I struggled to focus in class, though I did well on tests. If something interested me, I would read dozens of books on it, even after the class had moved on to other things. I was talkative and emotional.

The therapist had me fill out a checklist, which I was to bring back to the next appointment. It didn't take her long to tell me that I met the diagnostic criteria for ADHD—attention deficit hyperactivity disorder. I was skeptical. Wasn't ADHD a thing little boys had that made them react badly to sugar and red dye and bounce off walls?

> Wasn't ADHD a thing little boys had that made them react badly to sugar and red dye and bounce off walls?

Well, yes and no. ADHD is more complicated than that. Males and females can have ADHD, but males are more likely to be diagnosed and are diagnosed earlier than females. And boys tend to have more outward symptoms, while girls are more likely to be daydreamers, lost in their own thoughts. Instead of acting out physically, girls are often more talkative.[*] Both genders struggle with focus and organization. And it doesn't go away just because you turn eighteen.

Suddenly, I had a name for everything I had struggled with the previous four decades of my life. I felt vindicated, like a weight had been lifted from my shoulders. I wasn't defective, just different. My brain functioned differently, and my prefrontal lobe needed extra

---

[*] "How ADHD Shows Up Differently in Boys and Girls," APG Health Behavioral Healthcare, accessed January 27, 2026, https://www.apghealth.com/blog/difference-of-adhd-in-boys-girls/.

stimulation. That explained my high tolerance for caffeine. I lived on coffee, and it didn't keep me awake. It seemed to help me sleep.

An ADHD diagnosis didn't fix everything. In fact, it didn't fix anything. But it gave me clarity and helped me know where to start.

> An ADHD diagnosis didn't fix everything. . . . But it gave me clarity and helped me know where to start.

My doctor was hesitant to prescribe stimulant medication at first. This is common enough because doctors don't want to get in trouble for prescribing controlled substances. But I eventually found a provider who would give me the medications my brain craved.

With some coaxing from a friend, I went to an eight-week coaching group that taught me how to leverage my brain, how to use hyperfocus to my advantage and improve my executive function.

I found a therapist who understood the condition and coordinated with my doctor to help me find a safe, sustainable medication regimen. It's a process.

It wasn't easy. But armed with a new understanding of how I functioned best, I was able to tackle the issues at work with renewed hope. I can't say I was ever the model employee I would have liked to be, but with the help of my therapist and coach and my boss, I got off the performance plan long enough to get to the point where I could retire. My greatest fear had been that I would be denied my pension just when I got to my eligibility. I had intended to work a little longer. But the pandemic had forced us into working virtually, which I hated. And they were going to adopt a hybrid model, which meant I would have to learn my job a third time. I decided to leave on my terms, not theirs.

In the days after I got the diagnosis, I struggled with anger and resentment. Why did it take until I was at my wits' end and well into middle age for me to get the answer to so many questions? Why did my teachers, doctors, and therapists not put two and two together and figure out my issues?

> Why did it take until I was at my wits' end and well into middle age for me to get the answer to so many questions?

That's an easy answer, though. No one was looking for the right culprit. It's only been in the last twenty years or so that the medical community realized that ADHD lasts into adulthood and that women can struggle with it too. Doctors often assumed that the symptoms I experienced were the result of poor planning or hormonal shifts, not a different wiring of the brain.

In my life, ADHD has been a blessing. I knew that I wasn't suited for jobs that required long hours at a desk. And I found jobs that allowed me to do home visits and do many different things throughout the course of the day. I'm good in a crisis most of the time. And I'm creative and flexible. If I had been diagnosed as a young adult, I'm sure there were parts of my life that would have been easier. I might have avoided the improvement plans, and maybe I could have gotten promotions instead of lateral transfers.

I might also have avoided the massive credit card debt I had to fight my way out of. Impulsivity is a huge issue for me, and that helped lead to overspending. Even with the accountability I have in my life and the medication that I take every day, I still have to put limits on my computer time. I can't be on Amazon later in the evening after my medication has worn off or I might decide that a $1200.00 fountain pen is not only a bargain but a necessity.

But I would have missed out on a lot also. Hyperfocus can be a curse. I have lost hours and days to "rabbit holes" of interest. But because I have read broadly about a lot of different topics, I can find common ground with most people. There are few times that I am at a loss for things to talk about. I can converse about eighteenth-century revivalists, the American space program, fountain pens, or nose work training for dogs, just to name a few.

> My brain functions differently from many other people's brains. But different doesn't mean disordered.

Having ADHD has made me resilient and creative. I've had to find new ways to organize information. I can see things from more than one angle, and this means I often find creative solutions to problems that others can't see.

I don't like the "disorder" in ADHD. My brain functions differently from many other people's brains. But different doesn't mean disordered.

Faith Without a Safety Net

ANDREA GRIBBLE

IN NOVEMBER OF 2013, JUST days before Thanksgiving, I walked into my work as a product marketing manager, expecting a normal day. Thirteen and a half years on the job I'd held since graduating from college was long enough to believe that loyalty and hard work created security. I was a single mom with two amazing young daughters. I had a mortgage, responsibilities, and a life that, while not *exactly* what I had planned, felt solid.

Then I saw our vice president of operations standing at the door.

When you've been in management long enough, you recognize certain moments instantly. I knew before he spoke a word. My position had been eliminated.

It felt as if the air had left the room. My first thoughts weren't about my career or my title. They were about my girls. *How am I going to support them? How will I pay the mortgage? What am I supposed to do now?*

At the time, it felt like the end of the world.

I know now that it was the beginning of the greatest transformation of my life, but that perspective came much later. In the moment, there was only fear, anger, and disbelief.

Uncertain and Empty-Handed

When I walked out of the building that day, I walked out with nothing. My laptop was company-owned. My cell phone was company-owned. Thoughts swirled. *What do I do? Where do I go? How do I call anyone?*

One of my closest friends from work happened to be home on a day off, and she lived just a mile away. Distraught, I drove to her house, sat down, and tried to breathe through the shock. I needed to call family. I needed answers. I needed a plan that I didn't have.

Eventually, I pulled myself together enough to drive home.

I had to tell my daughters, who were nine and seven at the time. I tried to put on a brave face, telling them Mom wouldn't be going to that job anymore, that maybe this change would mean more time together. Inside, I was unraveling.

> Losing my job at thirty-five felt like being knocked flat on my back.

I had been independent my entire life. I'd built my own five-bedroom home on ten acres when I was twenty-four. My six-figure income was comfortable. Stability wasn't just something I had—it was something I *believed in*. Losing my job at thirty-five felt like being knocked flat on my back.

When Fear Met Calling

The uncertainty was relentless. But even in that fear, I felt a quiet nudge to keep moving. I started networking and looking for jobs. I said yes to conversations. One of those conversations changed everything. A female entrepreneur friend made a simple observation. "So many business owners are so busy running their businesses that they don't have time to do social media."

I didn't have a background in social media. I went to college for chemistry. But something inside me stirred. *Hey, I can do this. I can learn.*

There were blogs, podcasts, courses—resources everywhere. I didn't feel confident, but I felt willing. If I was going to bet on anyone, I decided I would bet on myself and trust that God would meet me in the effort.

Starting a business was exhilarating and terrifying. One morning I woke up thinking, *I'm my own boss.* A week later the reality also hit: *If there's no paycheck, that's on me.*

Unexpected Opportunities

The first real opportunity came through a connection I never could have planned. My mom worked as a district administrative secretary at a local school. She mentioned my situation to the superintendent. He emailed me and asked if I'd help the district with social media.

I said yes.

It didn't feel like marketing. Instead, it was celebrating students, teachers, and staff—telling stories of good things happening in schools. One school turned into another. And that was the beginning of #SocialSchool4EDU, the business I never could have imagined when I was studying chemistry.

I woke up excited about my work.

But excitement didn't erase reality.

Letting Go of Independence

Six months into my business, I had to face the numbers. When you start a business, you don't make much money at first. I couldn't afford my house anymore. That's when the anxiety really settled in.

Selling the home I had built from the ground up was devastating. It felt like letting go of proof that I had "made it." On the very day I was moving out of that house, I received a job offer.

It was everything logic demanded. A solid salary. Benefits. Vacation. Insurance. Security.

I sat down with Bill—who would later become my husband—and told him I felt like I had to take it. My family needed stability.

He looked at me and said, "You can always go back and get a job. But you can't start and stop a business like this."

At that point, I had just signed my third school client.

I decided to give my business six more months. If it didn't work, I could return to corporate life. But I wasn't done trusting God yet.

That decision changed everything.

> Amid it all, the right people continued to come into my life, and doors opened.

Amid it all, the right people continued to come into my life, and doors opened. And I decided, *Hey, if I'm going to bet on anybody, I'm going to bet on me, so why not just try this? What's the worst that can happen?*

Courage Amid What I Couldn't Control

Within a short time, I had eleven schools. I began hiring stay-at-home moms who needed flexible work. The vision became clearer. The direction made sense. But courage still came at a cost.

After selling my house, I moved in with my parents. At thirty-six. With two young daughters. That move forced me to confront my pride. I had been independent my entire life. Now I needed help.

I remember networking events where I couldn't afford lunch. My mom quietly left money on the seat in my car so I could eat with everyone else. The girls and I were on assistance for a time and had state-funded health insurance.

It was humbling in ways I can't fully describe.

My anxiety intensified. I sought counseling. Eventually, I needed medication to help manage it. I share that openly because resilience is not pretending that you're fine. It's choosing honesty and healing.

My parents are wonderful, and I stayed with them part-time for a year. I'm totally type A, so getting thrown on my back like that was hard. But everything I've learned has made me a better mom, wife, and daughter.

Through all of this, my daughters were watching. My four stepsons were there for the journey too.

They watched me lose everything I thought defined success. They watched me rebuild from nothing. They watched me choose courage when fear made more sense.

On the day when I told my oldest daughter we were selling the house she had lived in from infancy, she'd said, "Why don't you just ask for your job back?"

> "This is just a house. We are healthy. We have each other. And we are going to build great memories."

I looked at her and said, "This is just a house. We are healthy. We have each other. And we are going to build great memories." And we definitely did build them.

Years later, those memories became treasures.

I have tried to always instill in my girls that sometimes life is not what you had planned, but think of all the blessings that we have because it did end up this way. There's so much to be thankful for, people that you meet and experiences that you get to have and connections you get to make that never would have happened if it had happened any other way. I've tried to really lean into that.

I also lean into the fact that I'm not perfect, and God certainly knows that I try to be a little bit better every day. And definitely, as I grow closer to him, every day gets better.

What Resilience Has Taught Me

Looking back, I see how much that season shaped me. I learned that skills are transferable. That confidence grows through experience. The professional development—books, podcasts, conversations—can sustain you when money is tight. I listened to countless podcasts during that season because they were free and full of wisdom.

I believe in people so much, but you've got to be able to believe in yourself. And it's not easy, especially when you're living in your parents' basement and you can't buy a bottle of water or a pack of gum.

It took time, but eventually, I found myself serving hundreds of schools across the country. I now know that if my business disappeared tomorrow, I could build again. I didn't believe that at the beginning. I believe it now.

My life didn't turn out the way I planned. But it turned out fuller than I could have designed. Through marriage, my two daughters became part of a blended family with four boys. My work has meaning. My faith is deeper. My definition of success has changed.

If I could say one thing to the woman standing in that office doorway in 2013, it would be this: *It is worth it.* Even when you're walking by faith without a safety net.

A Bold Move

MEL TAVARES

I CROSSED THE RIVER AND KNEW my life would never be the same again.

There was nothing dramatic about the crossing itself. In my rearview mirror, I saw just an ordinary bridge arcing across the river. But sometimes the most ordinary thresholds are the ones that change everything. With every mile I drove, I felt something loosening behind me, like invisible cords snapping one by one: expectation, fear, obligation, guilt. By the time I reached my safe haven in southern New England, I was no longer the version of myself I had been for far too long.

Leaving my homeland wasn't a whim. It wasn't a dreamy adventure or a romanticized idea of a new chapter. It was a costly choice—emotionally, financially, spiritually. But it was also a necessary one. Sometimes survival demands a high price, and sometimes freedom requires a toll you never wanted to pay.

Marrying into a spiritually unequal relationship is one matter, but one spouse becoming a believer (Christ-follower) *after* marriage is quite another matter. My situation was the latter, and following Christ served only to further aggravate my world-loving husband.

For nearly two decades, I stood firm, believing and obeying the words of Scripture. "In the same way, you wives must accept the authority of your husbands. Then, even if some refuse to obey the Good News, your godly lives will speak to them without any words. They will be won over by observing your pure and reverent lives" (1 Peter 3:1–2).

> I did all I knew to do and was emotionally capable of doing in the midst of trauma.

Not that I behaved in a perfectly godly manner while under the duress of being in a less-than-ideal situation. I tried, often succeeded, and sometimes failed. My best explanation is that I did all I knew to do and was emotionally capable of doing in the midst of trauma, and I'm grateful for God's sustaining grace.

But the marriage that was supposed to be a partnership slowly became a cage. Not always loud but always controlling. Not always visible but always confining. Friends have since acknowledged they'd been concerned for years but never spoke up.

Surrender

Other Scripture spoke to me as well: "But if the husband or wife who isn't a believer insists on leaving, let them go. In such cases the believing husband or wife is no longer bound to the other, for God has called you to live in peace" (1 Corinthians 7:15).

After one especially painful night, something inside me finally broke open with my husband's words.

"I want a divorce. I'm tired of you, tired of dealing with kids. Done. I want a divorce."

When my now ex-husband demanded once again to be released from the responsibilities of marriage and family, I felt God whisper something I had been too afraid to hear: "Let him go. Step into peace."

With the surrender to finally agree to his decades-old demand for a divorce, I knew I was stepping into a new identity: single mom, responsible not only for my own future but for shaping a world of safety and possibility for my children. Fear of failing crept into my mind, but God was my ever-present help in my time of trouble.

Divorce is a word that weighs heavily in many cultures, including small villages where everyone knows everything, or at least thinks they do. Even friends at the small church lacked understanding and pried for details I refused to air. Questions. Probing. "Are you OK?" "Why did you take the kids and leave?" "After twenty-five years of marriage, you're just walking away?" "Did something happen I don't know about?"

Curiosity disguised as concern. And a sinking realization that explaining the truth would require peeling back layers of pain I wasn't ready to expose.

Sometimes silence is not secrecy—it's survival.

> Sometimes silence is not secrecy—it's survival.

Made for More

For years, I lived inside a life that felt too small for my soul. The people around me—the ones who were supposed to uplift, protect, guide—were becoming increasingly toxic. It wasn't always obvious. Toxicity has a way of dressing itself in familiarity and tradition, making you feel as if *you're* the problem for wanting more. There were voices telling me who I should be, what I should accept, how much I should sacrifice. There were subtle manipulations disguised as advice and controlling behaviors wrapped in the language of love.

The churches in the area felt lifeless. In too many cases, there was no passion, no movement, no true connection to God or his call to change the world. Just routine. Ritual. Pressure. It was a place that preached hope but seemed to live without it. And perhaps the hardest part: there was no vision. No dream for the future. No sense of growth or God's purposes. Just the expectation that I would stay quiet, compliant, small.

Too often I heard the question, "Why can't you just be content, like the rest of us?" When I expressed my desire to answer the call God had placed on me to become a writer, I was told, "People like us don't write books."

All of this existed inside a village that felt like a shadow of what it could have been. An oppressed place—*truly* oppressed. You could feel it in the air: the addictions that swallowed entire families, the whisper of witchcraft practices that lingered like a dark residue, the heaviness of hopelessness that sank into the soil that was once hallowed ground. It was a village where dreams didn't grow, where people stayed because leaving felt impossible, and where survival looked like repeating the same patterns generation after generation.

I remember driving through the streets after I'd relocated the kids and me to a new home nearby, and feeling as though the walls themselves were watching, silently daring me to try to escape. The area is the kind of place where people talk about freedom but don't believe in it. Where no one asks what you want from your life because they assume they already know the answer: Not much.

While my marriage was falling apart, my understanding of who God is was growing. I'd come to understand he has plans and a purpose for my life, and that it was OK not to be satisfied with the status quo. "When people do not accept divine guidance, they run wild. But whoever obeys the law is joyful" (Proverbs 29:18). In the King James Version, the wording is "where there is no vision." I was surrounded by people with no vision and no desire to seek divine guidance to answer the call of God and his purposes for them.

Have you ever been told you're "too much" or dreamed "too big"? Don't believe it for one moment. Small-minded environments cannot fathom or tolerate a God-sized calling.

> Have you ever been told you're "too much" or dreamed "too big"? Don't believe it for one moment.

It's strange how long a person can survive in an environment that steals the very breath from their lungs. We learn to normalize the weight on our chest, the buzzing under our skin, the exhaustion that never quite goes away. We tell ourselves it's not that bad. We tell ourselves others have it worse. We tell ourselves we don't deserve more, or that wanting more is selfish.

If you've ever walked on eggshells or shrunk yourself to survive, please know God saw every moment. You were never unseen or unloved by him.

I told myself all of those negative things because they'd been ingrained into every fiber of my being since birth. But then came the day when I could no longer be satisfied with the status quo. Something inside me—the part that had been quiet for too long—finally shouted loud enough to be heard: *This is not your forever.* Nor did I want it to become my kids' "forever" destiny. God had more for us.

So, I packed what I could. Hugged the pieces of our old life goodbye. And drove south.

I didn't cry. I didn't shake. But I felt the shift inside me, subtle and seismic at the same time. As I crossed the bridge, I kept thinking about my children and the eyes that would one day search for answers about how we ended up in a different world. I wanted to be able to tell the truth: that I chose freedom. That I chose peace. For me, but also for them.

Once safely in the "new land," nothing magical happened. The sky didn't open. The pain didn't dissolve. Life didn't suddenly feel easy, especially living in an RV in a campground instead of a house. But for the first time in a long time, I could breathe. Courage and boldness grew as we settled into a new life filled with laughter and music and freedom to be ourselves.

Leaving didn't mean everything became perfect. The cost still shows up years later—only seeing my family back in my homeland a couple of times a year, walking into a store and realizing no one knows my name, the financial strain of living in a more expensive state, the ache of rebuilding from scratch, the whispers of doubt that ask if I did the right thing. Kids who still struggle with the childhood trauma they endured. The many friendships that ended because I remained silent about details.

> Even with all of the struggles, I feel more alive than I ever did.

Yet even with all of the struggles, I feel more alive than I ever did in the place I left behind.

Because on this side of the river, there is vision. Possibility. Space to grow. An inner knowing that even if I don't have all the answers, at least I am free to search for them. I've become resilient. Strong. Unbreakable.

Bold New Beginnings

Healing happened, and in due season, God has brought me a wonderful man, a widower who loves Jesus and serves him and our family wholeheartedly. He supported my longtime desire to go to Bible school and to study and apply the Word of God. He was by my side when I was hooded after earning my Doctor of Ministry degree. I've answered the call as a writer and am writing books and articles, mentoring beginning writers, and teaching at conferences. I serve in my community and local church and am fulfilling the purposes for which I was created.

When I look back now, I realize something important: the river wasn't just a physical boundary between states. It was symbolic of everything I had to cross internally—the fear, the conditioning, and the pressure to stay small. Crossing it was an act of courage and faith in a future I couldn't yet see.

> I chose hope over despair, light over darkness, growth over stagnation. I chose to trust God to fix an impossibly messy life.

I chose hope over despair, light over darkness, growth over stagnation. I chose to trust God to fix an impossibly messy life. I chose to give my kids a life filled with hope and possibilities. I chose to break cycles instead of inheriting them. I chose to believe that my story wasn't finished—even if others tried to write the ending for me.

And now, on the other side of that river, my story continues.

What Grows Underground

MICHELLE RAYBURN

FOR TEN YEARS, THE DAFFODILS grew leaves but withheld their flowers.

I'd planted them in a season of transition when we moved our family to a new town. As we packed the boxes, I dug up a few clusters of roots from each of my beloved perennials to plant in our new yard. It was spring, the promise of new growth and flourishing, and the perfect time for dividing plants and propagating new soil.

Cardboard boxes of dirt clusters rested in the back of the minivan as I drove the two hours to our new town to meet up with the carpet installer just weeks before the move. I tenderly transplanted the shoots while he worked inside.

Soon, we transplanted the family too. And the foliage of succulents, lilies, and hostas emerged from the ground.

Over the years that followed, some plants thrived and naturalized. But the daffodils pushed through the last snow each year, bringing nothing but greenery before wilting in the summer sun.

Apparently, transplanted perennials don't always bloom on schedule, if ever at all. I figured they were adjusting to new soil and direct sunlight, or the jolt of moving them mid-season was just too much.

I knew transplant shock well.

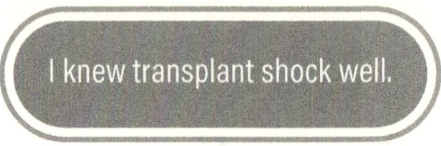

A Time to Plant

I was ten when my family uprooted and moved to a new town. New school. New church, and new friends. But it wasn't the perfect season for transplanting anyone or anything. Moving into unfamiliar soil in the middle of a school year was harsh in ways I couldn't put into words as a prepubescent youth. And outside of pen pal letters, there was no real way to stay attached to old friends.

Dad had always wanted to be a dairy farmer, and when they found the property, the purchase went through quickly. "You'll be in a new school after Thanksgiving break."

What? That was weeks away.

Barely time to say goodbye and finish making my Ponce de León puppet and give the conquistador report for our fifth-grade unit on Spanish explorers. There were forts to build at recess. *Important* stuff to finish. Attending a private Christian school also meant that some of my friends at school were at church every week. A family kind of connection. Therefore, much of our time was spent in one another's homes with kids playing hide and seek in the basement while adults played Rook upstairs. This was my whole world.

I was born in that town. My grandparents, aunts and uncles, and cousins lived there too.

It wasn't possible to fully process this sudden departure.

Moving day brought heavy snow as the afternoon wore on. After school, Mom navigated the one-hundred-mile drive on slick roads with us three kids, a cat, and four Siberian huskies in a commercial panel van full of tools and equipment, my dad's former work van, borrowed for hauling humans and critters. What a group of pioneers we were. Dad had gone up earlier because of farm stuff, leaving Mom to captain this vessel. The windowless rear of the van offered no view from my makeshift seat. (We survived those days of unrestrained trips in vehicles fitted with fewer seats than people like champs, didn't we?)

It was a fitting start for a rugged season.

Looking back, I can see how my parents struggled with the transition as well. Some Sunday mornings, my dad finished milking cows, and we squeezed five of us into a little Volkswagen for a two-hour drive to our old church—just to be near friends and family again. Dad's earthenware mug of steaming coffee kept the windshield frost-free, and those trips etched the scent of strong black coffee and his aftershave into my memories. We hurried home after lunch for the evening milking again.

A Time to Uproot

I transferred from one private Christian school to another, but that was about where the similarities ended. I want to report that I bloomed right away. That I made friends and fit right in. To say that the move toughened me, clarified me, made me adaptable and brave. But it wasn't so.

> I want to report that I bloomed right away.... But it wasn't so.

Just like that, I was the kid who went from a straight-A student to being clueless about what was going on in class. They weren't studying Spanish explorers. I failed a quiz on the bus boycott and Rosa Parks in my first week, not because I hadn't studied, but because I didn't know what to study yet. There's a particular humiliation in being tested before you've had time to orient yourself.

Fifth-grade girls aren't known for assimilating new friends either. This is the age where notes and rumors are passed around, and recess groups have castes. My response to feeling frustrated was, and still is, to cry. It's embarrassing still when I try to stop it, but tears are my first response to that feeling of not being in control of what's happening around me.

At night, silent tears spilled out of the corners of my eyes and trickled past my ears onto my pillow. I made up little songs about going back "home."

My younger brother and sister and I shared a makeshift bedroom in the farmhouse. Makeshift because the upper level wasn't inhabitable until the broken windows and crumbling plaster could be replaced. We lived amid renovations while my parents did the exhausting work of acquiring cattle and farm implements, then milking cows, plowing, planting, and harvesting, while remodeling a house in their limited free time.

The Years of Leaves

Anyone who has had to start over knows that it's complicated. There are moments that feel safe and comfortable, where a word of encouragement or praise becomes pure joy. Where one connection with a friend can make all the difference. Or where progress feels as tangible as winning a game of kickball, complete with high-fives all around.

In between making family memories and charting new and exciting paths are the moments with head in hands, sitting on the cold, stone steps, waiting for a ride after cheer practice, crumpled into tears of hopelessness.

I'll never make friends.
Nobody likes me.
I don't need anyone. I've got this on my own.
This will never get better.
I have to pretend I'm okay.

> It's a ping-pong of emotions, wanting to self-protect and participate at the same time.

It's a ping-pong of emotions, wanting to self-protect and participate at the same time. Yes, there are days of being vulnerable enough to let others in, brave enough to form new friendships, and tender enough to minister to other underdogs. But there will always be times when unhealthy self-preservation keeps us from bonding. Moments when never starting a friendship sounds safer than risking another loss. Where living with a mindset that every good thing eventually comes to an end sounds like a good idea instead of a ridiculous reason for not reaching out.

Those patterns can be established from youth, and we don't even realize it. I'll never know if my slow adjustment to an abrupt move created an easy-release connection on friendships for the rest of my life, or if I was a free spirit from the start. Was it my gravitation to the adults in the room rather than my peers that affected friendships? My introverted nature? Or was it that others didn't take a shine to my regular habit of tattling?

Yeah, I was *that* annoying kid. Miss Cries-a-Lot Tattletale Tuesday would have been my toy action figure name. I wasn't sporty or popular or trendy, but I was honest. To. A. Fault.

Looking back at the past could sound like a poor-me situation. Or it could be the best thing ever. In hindsight, I see that my mom and dad made a brave decision to do something unexpected, and I'm grateful they made that choice now. It's also relatable after having to walk in their shoes.

In our thirties, it was easier than expected—and I won't psychoanalyze that—to pick up and move after being quite firmly rooted where we were amid our parents and siblings. Our kids had grandparents and cousins, whom they saw often between school and church. That sounds familiar, doesn't it? History has a way of repeating itself.

But the real story is that beneath the surface, *some* growth is always happening. Every experience contains a mix of good and bad. And eventually, something shows for it. Solid evidence that something changed and grew.

> Every experience contains a mix of good and bad. And eventually, something shows for it.

We uprooted our family, following a similar pattern of my own lived experience, and moved two hours away. Sure, it was summer—not the middle of a school year—but my boys started over with new friends in middle school, not all that differently from what I'd had to do. New church, school, house, friends.

I carried a tenderness for their loss.

"We sense God leading our family here," we told them.

"I sense he isn't telling us that," one son said.

Oh, I knew that feeling. The one where you don't understand why your parents have a different picture of what's good for you than you do. When you think they have surely lost their ever-loving minds.

Starting over felt like an adventure though. A brave quest all our own. It didn't take long to see that we were thriving. The boys made friends. I did too. It started to feel like home. And all those perennials I'd brought as little clumps and shoots eventually multiplied enough to divide. Little passalongs for new friends and neighbors to propagate in their yards.

Blooming, at Last

When the daffodils finally bloomed, I almost missed it. There was no announcement—just buttery yellow blossoms on a few stalks one spring day where there had only been leaves for so many years. Some things grew slower than others. That's my story too.

I didn't suddenly become someone different. Nor did I arrive at a finished version of myself. Growth had been happening all along. Without my awareness. A whisper of something new. It's still happening. That's how I move, steady, cautious, but capable of starting over abruptly if needed. It isn't because I'm fearless. I just keep moving forward and making progress.

Wearing "No" Like a Badge

MARTHA KNIGHT

I WAS JUST A SKINNY GIRL of about twelve years old, and I loved going to court. I was usually accompanied by my younger sister, who couldn't wait to get off the slick wooden bench we shared. Her lack of enthusiasm did not deter me from absorbing the essence of the crowded courtroom on a Monday morning. I marveled at the large number of inmates who shuffled into the brightly lit courtroom, their chains clanking as they made their way in bright orange jumpsuits to appear before the judge.

My father, an attorney in the state of Indiana, would instruct my fidgety sister and me to find a seat on one of the many benches in the gallery and warn, "Don't say a word. If everyone here stands up, you stand up. If they sit down, you sit down. I'll find you when it's over."

I found it hard to believe so many adults were in big trouble! Drunk driving, shoplifting, drug possession—all had to appear before the judge. They all said they were sorry. I thought they were more sorry about getting caught and wondered what would happen when they finally got out of jail and had to catch a ride home.

One day it finally occurred to me that my father's choice of what I saw in the courtroom came down to "guilty by association."

Don't want to get arrested for shoplifting? Don't hang out with kids who steal.

Don't want to get arrested for underage drinking at a party? Find a different set of friends.

Don't want to get in trouble for smoking weed? Find something else to do.

I understood.

If I thought court was entertaining, and it was, I looked forward to the random visits the local chief of police would make to our home. The chief was a good friend of my father and would let me turn on the red and blue lights and sirens when I was still too short to reach the pedals. The wailer was the best! I decided that someday, I was going to drive a car just like his and find the "bad guys." As it turned out, accomplishing that dream was more difficult than I imagined.

> Accomplishing that dream was more difficult than I imagined.

Eventually I was old enough to start thinking about college and what I wanted to do with the rest of my life. It was 1972, and things, they were a-changing. Women were angry that they were not getting paid the same as a man for doing the same job. The glass ceiling was ever-present as far as opportunity was concerned, with men being promoted and women being denied.

I found myself recalling a babysitter who once asked me what I wanted to do when I grew up. I'd said, "Well, I think I'd like to be an astronaut and go to outer space!"

"Oh, I'm sorry, honey. Girls can't go to space," she replied.

WEARING "NO" LIKE A BADGE

"Why not?"

"Only boys can go to space. Girls have to stay home."

It didn't sound fair to me. "Well, I'm going. I drink Tang every day. That should count for something."

"You could be a teacher, or a ballerina, or a mom," she said.

"I'm going to space."

NO, IT DIDN'T HAPPEN. NASA needed people with better math skills than I had. I'd never had any ballet lessons, so that was out. I didn't want to be a teacher. And I wasn't ready to be a mom. What I really wanted was to become a police officer. The only problem was that the police department was not accepting women applicants right out of high school.

I decided to get brave and call the department and ask if they would consider hiring a female. It did not go well. I politely asked if the department would be hiring women anytime soon.

"No," he said.

"But what if that were to change? I asked.

"It won't."

"But it might," I returned.

"Listen, young lady. Are you at least five feet nine inches tall?"

"No."

"Do you weigh at least one hundred fifty pounds?"

"No."

"Are you male?"

"No!"

"Then you're not getting in!" And then he hung up on me.

Since I found this quite irritating, I mustered up my courage and called him back. When he answered the phone again, I politely asked, "And if a person were going to talk to someone other than you, who would they call?"

"I strongly suggest you don't do that," the man said. He hung up on me again.

I walked downstairs and found my father and asked him, "Dad, if I wanted to be a cop, is there any way you could get me in? You know cops and judges and legal people. Help me out."

He looked up from his newspaper and very firmly stated, "No. And no daughter of mine is going to be a cop."

Well, I thought, *I'm going to college, and I'm going to get a degree in SOMETHING. And then when the time is right, in maybe a few years, I'm going to go to the police academy and become an officer.*

I BECAME A DENTAL HYGIENIST, got married, had two beautiful children, and then the siren call to police academy started once again.

I finally approached my then-husband and asked him how he would feel about me going to a police academy for a few months.

He looked at me as though I was crazy and said, "Not only NO, but h---, no!"

He made it clear.

I decided, *When the kids are just a little older, I'll try again.*

I put the thought of the academy on the back burner of my brain and waited.

> I put the thought of the academy on the back burner of my brain and waited.

About two years later, a friend approached me and asked if I would be interested in becoming a store detective for a large retailer not far from my home. I figured that it was kind of like being a cop, so I agreed to be interviewed by the head of loss prevention. He said they would need to do a background check, and I needed to take a written test to see how honest I was. I passed with flying colors, and he said he'd get back to me.

After three days, I still hadn't heard anything from him. After a week, I finally called him back and asked if he had made a decision.

"I'm still pondering," he said. I reminded him that I had passed all the tests, so I was wondering why he just didn't hire me. I then offered to work for two weeks for free, and if I didn't turn out to be a good fit, he could fire me with no hard feelings.

"It's just that you're so small," he said.

I told him I knew they had training available for their detectives, and I was not scared.

"OK. You're hired, and I will be paying you for your work here. You're on probation to see how well you do in picking up shoplifters."

I did not see fit to tell him I had never done that kind of work, but in the end, I broke store records for my number of apprehensions.

Time passed, and a lot changed in my life.

AND THEN, IT HAPPENED.

A friend called and asked if I had heard that a new police academy was starting in October and wondered if I was interested. I could hardly believe it!

Two officers were taking applications in their tiny office when I stopped in to get the necessary paperwork to sign up. One of them asked me, "Are you here to get the paperwork for your husband?"

I almost laughed. "No. I'm here to get the paperwork for ME to sign up. Please tell me you're taking women."

"Oh, yeah. We are."

I almost cried. As it turned out, for reasons unknown, the sheriff's department canceled that particular academy and reset it for one year later. While that was disappointing, it gave me time to get in better shape physically.

I had not done any pushups since high school. I had to get stronger, faster, quicker. By this time, I was almost fifty years old. So, every night for a year, my supportive new husband and I ran a two-mile course he had laid out. The first time I tried to run it, I made it to the corner, one tenth of a mile. By the end of that year, I finally beat my husband home. He was a good coach! I found I was not particularly fond of pushups, but I needed to be strong, so I hired a trainer to help me get stronger in three weeks' time so I would be able to pass the physical fitness test. I ended up tearing a rotator cuff that would eventually need surgery to repair.

I prayed for strength and stamina every day before class, passed the timed runs and sit-ups, learned how to ground fight, and managed to jump straight up from a standing position the required sixteen inches. I was bruised from head to toe after defensive tactics, but I didn't care. The dream was heading for reality.

> The dream was heading for reality.

I had one last physical fitness test to go, and then it was on to graduation. We had to do twenty-five pushups. I knew that with a torn rotator cuff, it was going to be challenging, so I took several over-the-counter pain-reliever tablets before I went to class, hoping to just get through the final test. I completed fifty sit-ups, timed runs, jumps from a standing position, and managed to complete nineteen pushups. Unfortunately, the arm refused to work any longer and collapsed. I could not complete the required pushups. I was devastated and knew I had to complete the entire test, or I would not be able graduate.

The instructors were disappointed but assured me that I could heal up and try again next year. I figured I had gotten this far, so I kept on running at the gym and in the neighborhood and doing as much as I could to stay in shape. I missed my fellow teammates, but they sent me encouraging words and told me not to give up.

The months went by, and finally it was time to sign up again for the academy. Back to running, back to jumping, back to defensive tactics, and getting pepper-sprayed again. I had to repeat the entire course of training. By this time, I was fifty years old, old enough to be the mother of many of my classmates, which we all found quite amusing.

One of the happiest days of my life was when the instructors asked me to give the commencement address at graduation. Ironically, I shared the stage with a new female police officer who once picked up the shoplifters I'd apprehended and was also the first female to join the ranks of the local fire department. I served warrants, arrested cocaine dealers, and worked undercover with Vice and Narcotics. I gave speeches at local high schools about underage drinking. I worked on surveillance teams to wipe out gang activity, and I thanked God every day for letting me do what I had always wanted.

Five Words

CRYSTAL STALLMAN

I WAS STARING OUT THE WINDOW, watching the first snowflakes of the season tumble from the sky, when I heard the nurse's voice crackle through the phone, "You have a brain tumor." Five words that splintered my world—and started a journey I wouldn't trade.

When Everything Changed

I didn't know then how much those five words would rearrange my life, only that everything familiar suddenly felt fragile. In late October of 2011, I went to the ER after experiencing hearing loss and numbness on the right side of my face. While a CT scan revealed nothing, my neurologist scheduled an MRI to rule out a stroke. Late in the afternoon on the day of my MRI, I received the news that I had a brain tumor, a meningioma.

I felt as if a door had been slammed in my face as my mind ran through all of the possible outcomes. The nurse I spoke to said that most of the time, these tumors are benign, slow-growing, and rarely cause symptoms. I heard these "positive" things she was saying, but all I could focus on was "brain tumor." I was home alone with our two small children at the time, and I started making phone calls: to my husband, a prayer warrior from our church, my dad—and it all became a little more real with each phone call.

The next two months were filled with numerous hospital visits and tests, but doctors were cautiously optimistic. For a while, I felt relieved, knowing that at the moment, things were stable. However, shortly after Christmas, I began to lose sight in my left eye. First there were shadows in my peripheral vision. Then I lost the ability to see color, and within three weeks, I was nearly blind. To reduce any swelling around my optic nerves, I was put on steroids that left me dizzy, numb, and wired. I had to quit driving and lost all sense of independence.

> I was losing something I had never imagined living without.

Even surrounded by care, I was losing something I had never imagined living without. But I had such an amazing support group that I never felt alone. I would not have made it through without the prayers, phone calls, emails, and other encouragement from my family and friends. It seemed as though each time I sat down at my computer, there was an email from someone with a word of Scripture, a prayer, a story from their own times of troubles, or a song waiting for me. Just knowing that people cared and took a few minutes to reach out to me made all the difference as I struggled from day to day.

Learning to See What Matters

One day in the midst of it all, I looked at my son with just my left eye (testing, as I always did, to see what vision I had lost overnight), and I could not see his beautiful blue eyes. All I could see was a white blank face.

I was so sad. Not just that I could not see his eyes, but sad that I had not been thankful. I had to ask myself a hard question. Had I never thanked God for my vision when I had it? No, I don't recall that I ever had. This, of course, took me on a journey of thinking of all the things I had taken for granted. It's not that I had not been thankful for them—it's that I had never taken the time to thank God for them. And then I tried to tell myself that everyone takes things for granted. Everyone has moments of thanklessness. But I knew this was not about everyone else; this was about me being thankful, thanking God, so I could live life fully. Losing my vision didn't just change how I saw the world—it changed how I understood gratitude.

> Losing my vision didn't just change how I saw the world—it changed how I understood gratitude.

Only Today

When the future felt too heavy to imagine, I learned to shrink my world to what mattered most. It was hard for me to look ahead and see a future where things would be back to normal. Instead, I focused on what I could not do. I could not drive. I could not cook. I could not see well enough to care for my children the way I wanted to. I could not teach as I once had. Living in the world of "can nots" only made things worse.

But then a word of encouragement came from a friend who had struggled with disabilities most of her life. She suggested I ask myself a question: "What do you absolutely, positively have to do today? If you can do it, rejoice. If you cannot, try again tomorrow." That question became my daily prayer: enough strength for today, and trust for tomorrow.

When the steroids did not improve my vision, my neurologist referred me to a specialist, and on Valentine's Day, amid a blizzard, my husband and I made the trip to Rochester to find out what would come next. By the time we reached our destination, fear had given way to a quieter, steadier resolve. After a consultation with a neurologist and a neurosurgeon, it was determined that the tumor needed to be removed as soon as possible. Both of my optic nerves were wrapped around the tumor and stretched beyond recognition. If it wasn't removed soon, I'd lose vision in both eyes.

Right Where I Was Supposed to Be

On the second day in Rochester, we were on a 6:10 a.m. shuttle to the medical complex for yet another test. As I sat there looking out the window into the darkness, one question kept going through my mind: *What am I doing here?* At that moment, everything felt surreal. This was not where I was supposed to be. This was not what I was supposed to be doing. But it was God's plan. I didn't believe God caused the tumor, but I trusted that he was present in it. Somehow, even without answers, I sensed I was exactly where I needed to be. After all the tests and consultations, my surgery was scheduled for a week later, and we went home to prepare for this next step.

The next seven days were filled with making plans—plans for our children while we were away, lesson plans for the subs who would be teaching my classes, plans for after the surgery—and time. Just spending time with my children, trying to make everything as normal for them as possible.

I was suddenly fluent in a vocabulary I never expected to learn—brain tumor, neurosurgeon, MRI, craniotomy, vision loss. These things happened to other people, not to me. I didn't feel angry with God or question him. The tumor existed, and wondering why wouldn't change that. What mattered was trusting that God was present in it.

I was told the tumor had likely been growing for ten to fifteen years. I couldn't know when it began, but God did. He had seen every moment I couldn't, and he was caring for me long before I knew I needed it. Remembering that steadied me as we prepared for what came next.

> He had seen every moment I couldn't, and he was caring for me long before I knew I needed it.

The night before my surgery, I sat in our hotel room and wrote a letter to each of my children. I was praying for the best, but I wanted to be prepared for the worst. I was faced with the knowledge that my daughter, who was only two, might not even remember me. My son was five, and I knew his memories of me would fade over time. I wanted both of them to know how much they meant to me, how blessed I was to have been their mommy, if only for a short time, and how being their mommy had made me a better person. I saved the letters on my laptop for my husband to easily find if I didn't make it home.

The next morning, we checked in at the hospital at 8:45. My surgery was scheduled for 11:00. The more minutes that ticked by, the more scared I became. When I was wheeled off down the hallway while my family and friends stayed behind, I could feel the panic rise in my chest, and I could not stop the tears. I tried to pray, but the words wouldn't come. There was a moment when I was all alone, waiting to be taken to the operating room.

A nurse walked by and knew by one look that I was terrified. She came over and talked with me about why I was there, about my children, about life in general. She rubbed my shoulders and held my hand. She didn't have to do any of that. She could have just walked right on by, but she didn't. And I knew that God had played a part in this kind nurse who took the time to help put me at ease, to get my mind on something other than the painfully slow minutes ticking by.

And then, all too soon, I was in the operating room, watching the anesthetist put the mask over my mouth. I woke up four hours later to several nurses telling me to wake up. I opened my eyes and breathed a prayer when I could see clearly, out of both eyes. I was alive, and I could see—it was more than I had ever hoped for.

Recovery took time, but clarity—both physical and spiritual—came sooner than I expected. The doctors were amazed that my vision had returned immediately, but I knew, as all those who had prayed for me did, that it was not a surprise to God. This had been his plan all along.

I'm thankful that my life was changed by five words I never expected to hear. When I look at the scar and remember that journey, I know now that those five words weren't the end of my story. They were the beginning of learning how to live fully—one grateful day at a time.

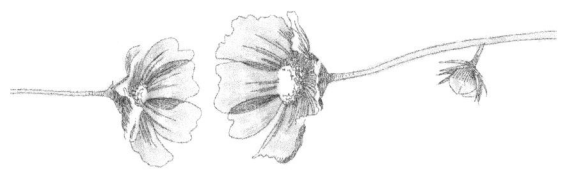

Hair Today, Gone Tomorrow?

KATHY CARLTON WILLIS

FINDING A GOOD HAIR STYLIST is similar to finding a mate for life. The search can bring about several one-date wonders on the journey toward connection. We women obsess about our hair. We want a stylist who understands our every desire. An easy style. Not only trendy but also face-flattering. Must do magic with our uncooperative hair. Many of us also want them to be color artists—the trusted supplier of the "fix" for our chemically dependent hair.[*]

The best way to find the perfect stylist is to find someone with a hairstyle you like and ask them which salon they frequent. When I complimented my friend Brooke about her new 'do, she referred me to Daniel. She said he was worth the trip out of town and gave me his number. I also liked the new hairstyle on my friend Linda, and she said she went to Daniel and gave me the address. I figured if two of my girlfriends like Daniel, he must be good.

I made my appointment and drove to Carlsbad, but Daniel said I wasn't on his schedule. After doing some investigation, I

---

[*] Parts of this chapter also appeared in *7 Trials Every Woman Faces* (Beaumont, TX: 3G Books, 2020), 87–104, by Kathy Carlton Wills.

discovered that Brooke's Daniel was in the opposite direction, in Roswell. There were actually *two* Daniels who styled hair!

Disappointed and deflated, I rescheduled. Sometimes when we are desperate for something, we end up jumping to the wrong conclusions.

> Sometimes when we are desperate for something, we end up jumping to the wrong conclusions.

Finally, the new appointment date arrived on my calendar. I made certain to get the address correct and ventured to the different town. This time, nothing would get between me and my hair's new style. I enjoyed my first "date" with him so much that I made an appointment for a total hair redo. My biggest hair adventure ever—foils! Again, I waited for the day, as if marking off dates on the Advent calendar prior to Christmas.

On my special renovation day, I jetted off to Roswell. During the drive, I daydreamed about my potential new look. Anticipation caused me to bolt out of the car into the salon. But to my dismay, Daniel was not in. He'd called in sick and couldn't reach me to reschedule. I had traveled forty-five minutes from Artesia for this? Others would have severed the relationship at that point, but not me. I was in pursuit of the perfect hairstyle. It was merely postponed—not out of reach.

I rescheduled *again*, and when I next met Daniel, we finally got it right. It was a hair partnership to "dye" for.

OTHERS CAN'T HELP BUT THINK of us based partly on what they see. They do not have the ability to read our minds or see into our hearts, so they study our physical appearance and our dispositions.

Sometimes all the brouhaha about our hair lives up to our expectations, and other times it doesn't. Daniel, *Brooke's* Daniel, did not disappoint!

Yes, I realize all this talk about hair is much ado about nothing. But first impressions and the opinions of others matter to us. "People judge by outward appearance, but the LORD looks at the heart" (1 Samuel 16:7).

A Different Kind of Disappointment

Other experiences have not always ended as well as the hair one. Years ago, I landed my dream job as a newspaper editor and enjoyed purchasing a professional wardrobe that was fitting for my new career. Every day I walked into my office with boosted confidence.

One day my boss asked me what time I planned to go home after work, so I told him, thinking it was merely small talk. About five minutes prior to my clocking out for the day, he entered my office with a box.

Something was terribly wrong.

> Something was terribly wrong.

He explained that the newspaper was having financial problems, and the rule for operating in the red was to fire the last one hired. That would be me.

"I'll give you five minutes to gather up all your personal belongings and put them in the box. I'll be back to escort you out of the building," he said.

True to his word, he returned and offered to carry my box to the car. He apologized for the security measures—he respected my integrity and the way I was handling being fired, but he was still required to do the walk of shame with me. As we made it to the car, he asked for my key and parking pass and wished me well.

Devastated didn't begin to describe my feelings! I had attached way too much importance to my identity as their editor. I recall driving through my tears. *I never saw it coming.*

Many disappointments in life are like that. Sadly, the newspaper didn't last too much longer.

We've all had to endure disappointment. As I think about it through the lens of resilience, I wonder which comes first, being disappointed or being resilient. It's a little of both, isn't it? As we develop the character trait of resilience, we can cope with disappointment better. When disappointment overwhelms us, it points out that something we'd hoped for didn't come to pass. We had good reason to believe it would happen, yet it didn't. Or an unwanted change happened. We learn to grieve the loss to move forward.

What does it look like to address the disappointment in a healthy way? I haven't always done that well! But I've learned I have to own the loss and not gloss over the unmet expectation. When I'm honest with how it makes me feel, I can address it in a way that allows for closure. It's taken a lot of years for me not to beat myself up for the way I feel when life goes differently than I hoped for. But now, instead of saying "emotions are bad," I've come to realize putting down emotions is dishonoring the way God created us. And it's not always even biblical when I try to brush it off by saying it must have been God's will.

> I've seen plenty of human error interfere with God's will.

I've seen plenty of human error interfere with God's will. (And yes, he allows the disappointing thing to happen, but it doesn't always mean it was for the best. God just makes it work out in the end.) These poor coping skills don't build resilience, and when I revert to them, I risk becoming bitter against God. This isn't a time to "fake it till you make it!"

Resilient people are hurt people who have learned how to develop a Christlike perspective. They heal with more insight for future challenges. Resilience grows as we learn not to attach our identity to outcomes or the approval of others. And it's expressed in beauty when we turn what we learn from it into compassion for others going through disappointing seasons.

Resilience isn't toughness. It's the ability to keep our hearts open for what is yet to come, rather than allowing ourselves to be discouraged and give up.

David Knew Disappointment Too

I've grown from seeing how David from the Bible dealt with people disappointing him. He was disheartened by their motives and actions—they tried (on purpose) to hurt him. What about us? Can we react like David? That's a trick question. Despite being let down by others, David praised the Lord. Even before our bad situations start to reverse, can we praise the Lord?

It must have disappointed David to do all he did and have others not come through when he needed them. If anyone had a right to ask, "After all I've done for you—you treat me *this* way?" it was David.

It's easy to get disappointed when real life doesn't measure up to our expectations. One of my checkpoints is to ask myself, will I play the victim, blame others, blame God, or find a way to work it out? Sometimes, when I process my options, I reframe my expectations and ask God to help me align my heart with his. When I get disappointed, it's often because I place my hope in something besides Christ alone. By anchoring my hope to God's character instead of my circumstances, I'm in the best place to ask God to equip me with what I need—even patience while I wait for it to get worked out. My tendency is to get ahead of God and force the situation, using my own abilities to get what I figure I have coming to me. But that way doesn't lead to contentment in Christ.

Any time I base my expectations on something outside my control, I set myself up for disappointment. Bank accounts can change. Family structure isn't set in stone. Even where I live or work or worship can be different during various seasons of life. If I invest my hopes and happiness in the promises or commitments of someone else, there's always a risk of having my heart broken.

When Expectations Go Unmet

My expectations of how others respond are usually based on how I think I would respond in the same situation—I expect them to have my same standard operating system. Often my expectations aren't realistic, and that's how I end up with them unmet.

Unfulfilled promises cause disappointment. The more others let me down, the more guarded I am with new interactions. I think I can mitigate future frustrations and disappointments by being less involved in relationships. And then, as I attempt to avoid new messes, my relationships become shallow and insincere. I certainly don't want that!

How have I gained wisdom and perspective? I seek God's principles for my relationships. God, our Creator, knows what makes us tick (and what makes the other person tick too!). We can look to him for advice on developing healthier relationships. He will inspire us to go on even when we manage to mess things up or they hurt us—again.

Rethinking Expectations

There's something to be said for lowering our standards! Let God be the one to set up the rules and regulations in the lives of others.

I have a hard enough time living up to the rules and regs God gives *me* to accomplish, let alone policing the successes and failures of others.

It's inevitable in life that we are going to get hurt. Others let us down. It's up to us to decide whether our expectations are unrealistic. We get a choice in how long we allow those feelings to be hurt or disappointed. Any time someone's actions and reactions are outside our control is an invitation to make sure our joy is not based on their choices. We set ourselves up for disappointment when we rely on others for our positive attitude.

> We set ourselves up for disappointment when we rely on others for our positive attitude.

We also get hurt when we don't meet *their* unrealistic expectations. Who likes to let people down! It's easy to feel judged a failure when this happens. Resilience has shown me that the best way to handle it is to ask what I need to do to make things right. I have the opportunity to strive to do better when it's in my power and ability to do so. If what they want is unfounded, then it's time to communicate why I can't measure up to their expectations.

Being disappointed is crushing. But it helps to realize God has equipped us to deal with our struggles. When we abide in him, we have access to nearly all of his resources. We can choose to concentrate on a new mindset. What happens when we point our focus where we want our hearts and minds to go? We develop more resilience for the next disappointment. And one thing we know for sure is, it's coming. But it doesn't have to destroy us. Or our hair!

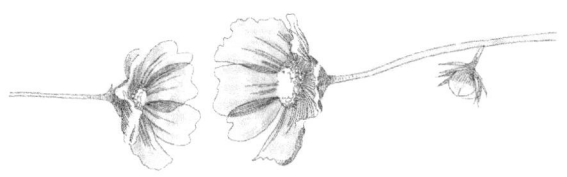

Burnout Was the Breaking Point

DIANA LEAGH MATTHEWS

"HELP ME! I CAN'T KEEP going this way." The cry came from deep in my soul. For years, I had been running at the proverbial thousand miles an hour. My body, mind, and spirit refused to continue at this pace.

Burnout wasn't a sudden collapse—it was seven long years of slowly emptying myself until nothing was left.

Recipe for Exhaustion

Seven years earlier, I had accepted a position as an activity director in a skilled nursing home. Beforehand, I'd worked briefly for another facility that criticized everything I did while offering no training. I stepped into the new role with something to prove—mostly to myself.

At first, I loved my new position. The residents captured my heart, and the variety of activities energized me. But the days were non-stop. I regularly worked nine- or ten-hour days, then went home to prep for the next day—cooking, sewing costumes, or pulling together crafts.

Evenings and weekends weren't downtime. They were for my writing, for learning the craft, chasing story ideas, and networking. Once a month, I also made the three-hour drive back home to help Mama care for my grandmother. Little of my life belonged to me anymore.

Perfectionistic Tendencies

I pushed relentlessly and scolded myself whenever something fell short of my expectations. I was harder on myself than anyone else could be.

Looking back, I can see how perfectionism masqueraded as faithfulness. I told myself that pushing harder was obedience, that exhaustion was proof of devotion. Rest felt selfish. Slowing down felt like failure. I believed that if I just did more—worked longer, planned better, tried harder—everything would finally feel "enough."

> My worth became tied to productivity, approval, and performance.

What I didn't recognize then was how deeply those beliefs were shaping my identity. My worth became tied to productivity, approval, and performance. When things went well, I felt momentarily validated. When they didn't, I internalized the failure. Resilience, I would later learn, was not about enduring at all costs, but about learning when to stop, listen, and trust God to carry what I could no longer hold.

For a season, I had a great assistant and administrator. But when my assistant retired and a new administrator arrived, everything changed. His lack of support—and sometimes outright sabotage after months of planning—chipped away at my confidence. My perfectionism only grew more intense. I worked harder, longer, faster, hoping to prove I was capable.

After four years, exhaustion settled into my bones, yet I kept pushing. I began the online certification programs, two 1200-hour director courses, followed by my consultation certification. I pushed myself to complete all three programs within less than a year. Surely this would show my boss I knew what I was doing.

Leaning on God

By the time I finished, I was mentally fried. No amount of rest restored my strength.

As a single woman, I had no one else to lean on. The bills had to be paid, so I kept going through the motions, even when my heart wasn't in them.

By year five, I cried on the drive to work without knowing why. With only a ten-minute commute, I barely had time to push the feelings down before plastering a smile on for the residents.

The workload didn't slow. With 120 residents to serve, each day included meetings, visits, documentation, and four to eight activities. Add in monthly holiday celebrations, birthday parties, outings, proms, pageants, and a family-wide Thanksgiving dinner, and exhaustion became my constant companion.

Christmas was the most demanding. Fundraising occurred year-round. By August, we were planning, scheduling youth groups to help decorate our twenty-seven trees, organizing performers, putting on Santa's workshop, baking cookies, not to mention pictures, gifts, and two enormous Christmas parties. I loved seeing the joy on the residents' faces, but each year I moved a little slower. My back and knees ached. My energy faded. Caffeine and electrolytes became my lifeline. My diet suffered. So did my attitude.

Depression wrapped itself around me. When I took even a small moment for myself—like getting my hair or nails done—I felt guilty. Something had to give.

I searched for other jobs, but nothing fit. I clung to the old saying: "Better the devil you know than the devil you don't."

So I pushed harder. But the harder I pushed, the worse my health and mood became. Then COVID-19 hit and added more demands and stress, pushing me past sanity and my limits.

I cried out to God more times than I can count, pouring out my weariness and begging for strength just to get through the day. One morning, I whispered, "Help me, God. I can't go on. I need a six-month break, but that's impossible."

Then, corporate announced they were selling. A pit formed in my stomach. Even though promises of good things came, my intuition said otherwise. The day before the takeover, I was called into the administrator's office. We agreed it was time for me to leave. I qualified for unemployment.

Those next six months weren't restful. My grandmother declined, and I moved back home. My days were filled with caregiving, packing, and constant trips back and forth. This wasn't the rest I had prayed for, but I kept going. My family needed and depended on me.

> That season forced me to confront a hard truth: burnout doesn't end simply because the job does.

That season forced me to confront a hard truth: burnout doesn't end simply because the job does. It lingers in the body, the mind, and the spirit. I was learning that rest is not just the absence of work, but the intentional rebuilding of what has been depleted.

I had to relearn how to listen—to my body when it ached, to my emotions when they surfaced, and to God when he nudged me toward stillness instead of striving. Some days, resilience looked like just getting out of bed and showing up. Other days, it meant saying no without explaining myself or allowing silence where noise once lived. Healing was slower than I wanted, but it went deeper than I expected.

Breaking the Cycle

Eventually, I accepted a job in hospice as a volunteer coordinator. The work was similar in some ways, different in others, and at a slightly slower pace. Over time, the heaviness of burnout began to lift.

But it didn't happen automatically. I made intentional changes—improving my eating habits, exercising more, carving out time for friends and family, and giving myself permission to rest. I began to take time for myself. Slowly, I felt human again.

Still, the health issues lingered. My knees worsened. Diabetes set in. Many evenings, all I could do was collapse. I stepped back from various groups and commitments, learning—sometimes reluctantly—to recharge instead of overextending.

Turmoil and turnover became constant at work, and after three years, the familiar signs of burnout reappeared. My creative well dried up. Writing—my refuge—became impossible. I hardly recognized the woman I'd become after a decade of constant striving.

Once again, I cried out, "Lord, help me. I can't keep going like this. I surrender all."

And this time, I meant every word.

Strength in Surrender

The following Scripture became my anchor: "Trust in the Lord with all your heart; do not depend on your own understanding. Seek his will in all you do, and he will show you which path to take" (Proverbs 3:5–6).

I clung to this truth when I was weary, discouraged, and unsure what came next. Each day, I made conscious choices to care for myself, failing more than I succeeded.

Then, in a way only God could orchestrate, the hospice company closed in our state, and another job opened at the exact same time. A position caring for troubled teens. Something completely new, completely unexpected.

I don't fully understand the why, but I choose to trust. Again and again, God had guided me through seasons where I couldn't see the road ahead.

> Again and again, God had guided me through seasons where I couldn't see the road ahead.

Today, life moves at a gentler pace. I'm rediscovering the creative parts of myself long buried under exhaustion. Friends tell me they see the change—lighter, happier, smiling again.

I'm finally slowing down enough to listen to the Lord instead of my own drive to perform. This healing journey hasn't been easy. It has required peeling back painful layers, confronting lies I believed, learning to care for myself, and facing my perfectionism. Often it means taking one step forward and two steps back. It has required prayer, honesty, and conversations with trusted friends.

In the process, I'm discovering who I am and about the person that I've buried under perfectionism and striving for far too long. This is also a time when I'm seeking what the future holds and God's plans for my life.

I am beginning to understand that resilience is not a one-time victory, but a daily practice. It is choosing faith over fear, rest over relentless effort, and obedience over control. There are still moments when old patterns resurface—when I feel the urge to prove myself or push beyond healthy limits.

But now, I pause. I pray. I ask better questions. I remind myself that my value does not come from how much I produce, but from whose I am. That shift—small as it may seem—has changed everything. It is teaching me how to live with intention instead of urgency, and trust instead of anxiety.

Finding Direction Again

True resilience is not self-reliance but trust—trusting God to meet us in our weakness and guide us when we cannot see the way forward. Though my story is still being written, hope has replaced despair, and faith has replaced striving. When I find myself exhausted and overwhelmed, I bring my weariness to the Lord. I lay it at his feet, asking for his direction and allowing him to show me the next step. I may not see the full path yet, but his light will be enough for today.

Anchored in His Presence

ALMIRA MICHELE ROBINSON

I STARTED TO SLOW DOWN AND wondered, *Is it menopause?* So, I was told.

I saw an apothecary. He created an iron supplement and prescribed vitamins. I got a temporary burst of energy, then went back to feeling draggy.

During that time, our little gray-and-white terrier, Jazz, chased a cat across the street. The cat skirted to the other side and survived, but not our Jazz. On Christmas Eve, disheartened and weary, I did not have it in me to attend service. I was the Christian school chaplain, among other things. I needed to be there, but I couldn't go on like this. I wondered, *What is wrong with me?*

January rolled around, and I was still not myself. Getting out of bed was difficult, and perseverance had run out months before. However, I was a US citizen working in Canada with no healthcare until my probation period ended in June, so I hesitated to go to the doctors. Plus, my prior four surgeries aided my decision.

On January 18, 2010, the pastor I worked for made the decision for me and drove me to see Dr. Quinn in another town. I call him the Medicine Man. Dr. Quinn prescribed antibiotics, thinking I had the flu. After the visit, the receptionist returned my payment for the office visit—per the doctor. Tearfully grateful, I knew God was up to something. On the drive back, God dropped Psalm 91 into my heart. This psalm became my anchor.

The flu-like symptoms continued. On Thursday, March 4, 2010, I awoke to a walnut-sized lump under my left arm. After many tests, including a mammogram, the medical professionals still did not know what was wrong.

The lump grew to the size of a grapefruit by April, and I had a painful biopsy with no anesthesia. *Why God?* I asked as I watched blood drip down my side everywhere.

On Monday, May 10, 2010, I received a call at work from my doctor to come to her office right away, with the suggestion to bring someone. *This does not sound good*, I thought.

> I knew it was bad when two doctors entered the room to tell me.

I knew it was bad when two doctors entered the room to tell me I had cancer. "An oncologist will call you by the end of the week for testing."

As the director of food services for an international nonprofit, I dragged myself to work on Tuesday, only to be driven home by the custodian because the pain was too much to move or stand. This was my last day of work.

I got the oncologist's call on Wednesday, and I met with him on Thursday for testing. I returned Friday, May 14, for additional testing and was diagnosed with a rare case of Burkitt non-Hodgkin lymphoma. The doctor said, "You will probably not go back to work again. Get your affairs in order. Pack a bag and meet me at the hospital on Monday. You will have a bone marrow aspiration, and we will start chemo on Wednesday. Do not search the internet."

Get my affairs in order in two days? What do you mean? I was seeing a naturopath at the time and had reservations and questions about chemo. "Can I pray first and let you know?"

"You don't have much time. You have cancer in your entire body, and it is growing fast. In about three weeks, you will be dead."

But I am only forty-seven?

THE NEXT DAY, MY FIRST grandchild was born. My first quest, rolling into the hospital, was to see my grandson before I checked in at oncology. The joy of seeing my grandson born to my teenage son and his girlfriend was mixed with emotions. (I didn't mention that after I'd found the knot, I learned she was pregnant a few days later. Because I was on the school's advisory board as chaplain, I was also part of the disciplinary actions of putting my son out of school in the eleventh grade.)

The inexpressible joy of the moment of meeting my grandson mended our hearts and gave me something I needed. Hope. I kissed and prayed a blessing over him, wondering if I would see him again. From that day forward, I called him my lifeboat.

> I kissed and prayed a blessing over him, wondering if I would see him again.

The hope of seeing him grow up got me through some very tough days. When I didn't want to endure anymore, my grandson would arrive on a surprise visit with his parents, put a smile on my face, and give me the courage to press through. The providence of God.

THE ART OF RESILIENCE

MY FRIEND CHERYL ROLLED ME to have a terrifyingly painful bone marrow aspiration to see if the cancer was in my bones. The anesthesia did not work. I felt the drill pierce my skin and bones as I screamed and clenched my friend's hand through the curtain. Because of other issues, the doctor sent me to see a gynecologist.

The next day, doctors discovered I had endometrial cancer.

My body was not in the condition for surgery because the lymphoma would kill me first. The medical team came up with a protocol with the hopes of getting me into remission. The Tuesday night before chemo began, I prayed, *God, I am your daughter and servant. Why is this happening to me?*

That night I was in excruciating pain, and the nurse came in to give me pain meds. She paused. I screamed.

Under my arm, I felt the sensation of being cut open with scissors, a huge hand reaching in and pulling something out, and the sensation of being sewn up with a needle. Immediately, the pain stopped.

The knot was gone. God had removed the lump, and he made sure there was a witness.

> God had removed the lump, and he made sure there was a witness.

After taking prep meds for the next day's chemo, I slept peacefully for the first time in a year. I awoke the next morning thinking, *I'm going home.* Instead, hospital staff surrounded me and stood staring.

FROM THAT DAY ON, I was "the miracle girl." However, the miracle girl was not going home.

Early morning scans revealed I still needed the treatment. Devastated, I asked, God, *Why?*

I reached for my Bible, praying. When I opened it, my eyes landed on 1 Peter 1:6–7.

> So be truly glad. There is wonderful joy ahead, even though you have to endure many trials for a little while. These trials will show that your faith is genuine. It is being tested as fire tests and purifies gold—though your faith is far more precious than mere gold. So when your faith remains strong through many trials, it will bring you much praise and glory and honor on the day when Jesus Christ is revealed to the whole world.

Two weeks later, after my first round of chemo, I was sent home. I wanted to do something normal, so I paid bills. Then, I licked a stamp.

Fifteen minutes later, I got a fever. I was rushed to the emergency room and then spent nine months in the hospital because of an infection from the glue. By February of 2011, I was allowed to return home to recover and prepare for surgery in June.

I received permission from the doctor to travel to the States to see my youngest child graduate from high school in Baltimore and fly to California to see my oldest son's Master's recital, since I would be unable to attend his graduation. I returned to my Canadian home and drove straight to the hospital for pre-op and surgery the next day. Only the Holy Spirit gave me that strength because Tired became my first name.

DUE TO THE CONDITION OF my body, my recovery from a full hysterectomy was longer than normal. My 2011 Christmas "present" was that the lymphoma had returned. Back to the hospital for additional rounds of chemo and spinal taps. My only option was to get my body in remission and receive a stem cell transplant. Since a donor match could not be found, God performed another miracle. An experimental drug financed by a Canadian nonprofit was used to produce stem cells from my already broken body, which were collected over a series of months, for a stem cell transplant.

I was told, "The seven days of high-dose chemo prior to the transplant will bring your body to near death. We will inject the stem cells and isolate you for one hundred days because you will have no immune system."

After that news, I was beside myself. My spirit was now broken. Knowing what I had already been through and the days of excruciating pain and chemo in my spine, I wanted to give up and die. I did not want to do this. I was afraid.

This was my first panic attack. I had moments like the day after my first spinal tap and the intense days of pain from the infection, but how would I emotionally survive? I was the strong one. I could not do this in my strength. I had none. Exasperated, I told God I was done.

> I could not do this in my strength. I had none.

Three friends came to visit, one after another. My first friend could not console me. She left. My next friend arrived and could not get me to stop babbling. No success in comforting me. I was forty-nine and felt like I was eighty years old. She left, and my third friend showed up with the ministry of presence. I was hyperventilating and angry. It all seemed unfair and made no sense. *Why would God remove the knot and let me suffer?* I cried, *Lord, how long?*

After the release of tears, fears, anger, and frustrations, my breathing returned to normal. My friend left. Maybe I needed that release? I grabbed my Bible, journal, iPod, and earphones and sat on my front porch for the last time of 2012. I took three deep breaths. My heart calmed. With earphones in, I pressed play. With no selection of a song by me, "Alpha and Omega" by Israel and New Breed played.

With that song, God reminded me of who he is, was, and will ever be—Alpha and Omega, a promise keeper. Psalm 91 came to mind just as it had when it all started, which he repeated in several ways through this trial. My friend Cheryl taped it in my room and on my chemo pole. I reminded myself, *I must continue to hide in the shelter of his wings and rest in his shadow. He is my refuge, strength, and place of safety, and I must continue to trust him.*

> God reminded me of who he is, was, and will ever be—Alpha and Omega, a promise keeper.

He was my faithful armor and protector and the remover of the knot that night in 2010, my visible anchor of promise for my weary soul. He knew the journey, and this moment would come when I needed assurance. He knew I would be exacerbated and exhausted. He was going to get me through.

Peace came.

September 20, 2012, was transplant day. It was unspeakably brutal. One hundred days later, I came home with twenty-seven medications, a pinched nerve, neuropathy in my hands and feet, and chemo-induced cardiomyopathy. Yet I am still here.

The doctor had said, "Twelve years from the stem cell, you will one day wake up and feel like yourself."

Now thirteen years later, that day has yet to arrive and may never, but I am persevering. I am on two medications. I can bend to tie my shoes and lift my arms to comb the little bit of hair that grew back—evidence of some freedom. He gave me joy amid the trial.

My son married his high school girlfriend, and I have five beautiful grandchildren. My first grandson is now fifteen. God sustained us financially. He kept a roof over our heads, and my children finished college and graduate school on disability income.

I have mourned my old self and life.

I don't feel eighty anymore. I do feel my age of sixty-two. I lost a lot but gained much more—mostly a trust and faith that is more precious than gold. God is restoring and giving me a new sense of purpose and joy in telling others about his goodness, faithfulness, and healing power.

Love

God's Intentional Interruption

JONI TOPPER

NO ONE IN THE ROOM spoke. It was a holy moment. Each team formed to serve inside the women's prison began with intensive training for the volunteers. By the time we heard those prison doors slam behind us, we were a family, a team, bound by a commitment to serve.

Our motto—Listen, Listen, Love, Love.

I STOOD IN LINE WAITING for my turn. The entire team stepped up one by one, each washing another member's hands, then praying over them. After my own were washed, I stepped forward to wash the hands of the next servant in line and offer a prayer for God's presence in their ministry.

A little red-headed boy about seven or eight years old burst into the room with his big green stuffed dinosaur tucked under his arm. I could see his mom trying not to smile and at the same time trying to quietly direct him away from the line he'd just barged through, the people waiting for their turn to wash their hands. She hoped to preserve the holiness of the atmosphere.

The whole team had seen him come in and out all day. We engaged the children of team members, knowing that sometimes single parents don't have any choice but to let their children tag along. The team-building meetings were mandatory for anyone who wanted to serve.

The little boy's mom signaled for her son to come closer. She used two fingers, pivoting between her own eyes and his, indicating he should come close and get eye to eye with her. He moved toward his mom, coming nose to nose with her. But his eyes looked to the ceiling and swiveled to the left, to the right, anywhere but eye to eye with Mom.

I resisted the urge to burst into laughter. He was so cute, and so was his mom. She wanted to be serious, but he was too adorable to be mad at him.

> I wondered how many times God has tried to get my attention eye to eye.

I wondered how many times God has tried to get my attention eye to eye, and I've looked up, down, and all around, anywhere but where he directed me to look. You know, those moments he tries to be intimate with us, but we just refuse because we have other plans.

The Scripture read just before the handwashing ceremony came from Jesus's experience with his disciples the day he washed their feet. Jesus said to them, "You don't understand now what I am doing" (John 13:7). Those words catapulted me to a memory from a few years ago when a crisis of faith shifted my plans, resulting in my presence at this very training.

GOD'S INTENTIONAL INTERRUPTION

Shifting to Retirement

For thirty years, my work at the post office provided my family's insurance and occupied a lot of my time. I can't tell this story without saying how grateful I am to have received the security it provided all those years. However, having expressed my gratitude, I must admit, retirement seemed like the chocolate cake at the end of the rainbow. My future looked bright. No longer would my days start at 5:00 a.m. Monday through Saturday, and I couldn't wait.

My last day of work would be May 24, 2017. If I could just coast through 2016 and endure the last Christmas season at the post office, the hard part would be over.

> I had envisioned having fun with her when I retired.

On December 13, 2016, I learned that my mom had advanced-stage cancer. Fourteen days later, she died. A major part of my retirement plan vanished with her. Mom lived 300 miles from me. For thirty years, I'd worked six days a week at the post office and served as the worship leader at the church my husband pastored on Sundays. I had envisioned having fun with her when I retired. I imagined a relaxed time when we could vacation, shop, go to women's retreats together, cook, and play with my grandchildren.

But she died five months before I retired. It's not that we never spent time together while I was employed, but it was always rushed and felt like stolen moments. I longed for spontaneous adventures with her.

My other expectation for retirement involved music. For twenty years, I'd spent hours every week working on music with a friend. He played guitar, and I played the keyboard. Our vocals blended beautifully, and we easily swapped back and forth between the lead parts and harmony. We sang at our church, at local events, for the National Park Service, at dedication services for other churches, for parties, around campfires, and anywhere music fit into the agenda. I called him my musical brother.

We made two CDs and began working on a third album. Completing that project topped my to-do list upon retirement. Then we would start another one. Several of the songs we recorded were originals; we wrote them together.

Two weeks after mom died, he picked up his guitar as he left church Sunday morning and said, "You will be fine without me. You did this long before I was around." I did not understand why he said that.

He never came back again. He decided to use his talent in the country music industry. We never had a conversation about it. He was just gone.

Unwelcome Detour

To say that I was bewildered would be an understatement. Everything I did with music was connected to him. I grieved Mom, I grieved my musical brother, and neither of their absences made any sense to me.

> I grieved Mom, I grieved my musical brother, and neither of their absences made any sense to me.

To withstand both losses at the same time seemed more than I could bear. Sometimes I came in on Sunday mornings to prepare for the worship service, and I would start crying but could not explain why. It required everything within me not to sob uncontrollably those days. God's sovereignty in the matter did not help me absorb my complete overwhelm at these losses.

Jesus's words to his disciples just before he died were as real to me as if he had spoken them directly to my situation. I did *not* understand what he was doing.

Changing Lanes

One of the last things Mom ever gave me was a guitar. When she brought it to me, I asked her why. "But Mom, I don't know how to play the guitar."

"You use your music, Joni, and your sisters don't play either. It just makes more sense for you to have this." Mom's logical answer satisfied me.

A few weeks later, after discovering the value of the instrument she left in my possession, I recognized that I should at least attempt to learn how to play it. I took lessons from a gifted young guitarist and enjoyed the venture.

> I took lessons from a gifted young guitarist and enjoyed the venture.

Not long into my guitar-playing days, my son married a woman whose young teenaged son also played. He and I led our youth group each week, and the teenaged girls thought he was the berries.

I carried the rhythm guitar part, and he added all the fancy riffs to make the music come alive. Playing together helped make bonding between us happen faster. Connecting with a teenager as a grandparent when you did not know the child from infancy is not always easy. I was thankful for this love of music that we shared. In my heart, I knew that if my musical brother and I had been deeply involved in a recording project, I might have been too absorbed with recording to connect with my new grandson so easily.

THE ART OF RESILIENCE

Then one day, someone came to me at church with an SOS for musical help in a women's prison ministry. I decided that it might be just the push I needed to improve my skills on the guitar. The actual words they used were, "They are desperate for a music team." I concluded that if they were desperate, they would likely think my contribution was wonderful.

The first rehearsal was two hours from my hometown, so I loaded my instrument and headed out for my first gig playing guitar. When I arrived, I discovered a very talented vocalist who did not sing any harmonies and a woman who was trying to learn the piano. In reality, she was an accomplished guitar player. Since I could sing either lead or harmony, stepping into the vocals was easy.

The other instrumentalist and I played a couple of songs in that rehearsal and then gave one another a sober look. "We need to change instruments, don't we?" I said to her. We laughed and swapped places. She took the guitar, and I sat down at the keyboard. Both of us were back in our comfort zones, and the music soared from adequate to excellent in about four measures.

Loving the Journey

I've been serving on the music team inside the prison with that vocalist now for several years. Our compatibility and skills are unique and wonderful. We sing in the prison ministry and for numerous other events. Then when I cofounded a women's event in my hometown, I did not have to search for a worship team. Just a phone call to my friend secured her faithful presence.

Worship inside the prison is like nothing I've ever experienced. It's hard to even put into words. The women sing with abandon. Their faces match their voices. Where sorrow and defeat walk into the room on their expression, as the music begins, it is replaced with hope and purpose. It always surprises me that they seem to know every song. They sing as though they've been suppressing the melody all their life and the tune just broke through the barriers.

Oddly, in that otherwise dark place, when we walk through those doors, the Holy Spirit does some powerful work. I've wondered many times if my musical brother had not moved in another direction, would I have gone there? After all, prison is not a place most people ever long to go.

God replaced my musical brother with a musical sister. My musical brother is still a beloved friend who is using his talent in another arena. God filled the gap in my heart that longed to worship using the best of my talent with another skilled musician.

> He transformed my broken heart and gave me a new melody.

In the process of experiencing this joyful connection unfold in my life, I have been reminded that God is trustworthy. He transformed my broken heart and gave me a new melody amid the very circumstance that I thought might be my undoing. I've learned that I don't need to know what he's doing. I just need to know that he's faithful and intentional. Right in the middle of what looked like an interruption to me, he gave me a song I didn't expect in a place I couldn't imagine, and it all seemed so natural. I think he planned it for good all along.

From Tattoo to Titanium

CHARLAINE MARTIN

"WOULD YOU REMOVE THAT IF we were to date regularly?" the man across the table asked, referring to my tattooed wedding band. He seemed guarded, apprehensive as he waited for my answer.

A twinge of pain struck me. "Only for the right man," I replied. After a moment, I looked into his eyes, wondering why my permanent band bothered him. "It's my only tattoo," I added, hoping to reassure him that I wasn't hiding any more body art.

"I see." He seemed to close me off, as if a red flag popped up in front of my face.

After dinner, he paid the check, and we each went our own way.

Sigh. He seemed nice. I really didn't want to begin dating as a mid-lifer; this situation wasn't my choice. God took my husband Home at fifty years old. We were supposed to grow old together. Now, I found myself searching for God's man for me to spend the rest of my life with, but now it was a matter of finding the right one.

My tattooed wedding band became both an opportunity and a challenge as I navigated the dating world. I always explained its meaning—my deep commitment to marriage. Yet my dates often saw it as a mark of ownership, creating a barrier to new relationships.

To understand how that small circle of ink came to carry so much weight, I have to go back to the day it was created.

A Lifetime Mark of Commitment

"How can I help you?" the biker dude tattoo artist looked at us through his round-lensed, steampunk spectacles as if we must be in the wrong place. Obviously, we were out of our element. Conservatively dressed, we were a total contrast to the usual clientele who frequented this establishment.

"We have an appointment with Cindy," my husband replied as I cautiously scanned Cin on Skin's tattoo shop.

The man, covered with tattoos peeking out from under his black leather vest, looked like a walking pierced jewelry and skin art display. He peered over the top of his glasses and inquired, "Who referred you to us, if you don't mind me asking?"

"A friend at work told us we should see Cindy for our wedding band tattoos."

> "A friend at work told us we should see Cindy for our wedding band tattoos."

"Oh, okay. Do you have a sketch?" His guard lowered as he examined the cross with two small diamonds on each side that we had found in a computer graphics manual. He smiled. "Yeah, she can do this." Scanning it on his flatbed scanner, he waved us back. "Follow me." With the copy in hand, the man led us down a hallway. He pulled back the cardinal red curtain for us as we entered the room; a stylist's chair with an armrest and a ball on its end awaited us.

"Hi! I'm glad to meet you. John told me all about you, Pastor Don." A cheerful, life-worn older woman, also a walking skin art gallery, picked up a tray of inks and tools for our session from the counter and brought them over with her gloved hands.

My husband was first in her chair, sitting back and resting his hand on the ball of the armrest. Immediately, his face turned pale as she brought the lightly buzzing needle over to begin her work. I thought he'd pass out as she carefully worked on his small skin canvas. He hated needles of any type that could enter his body, or mine. But the incentive of preventing his work equipment from damaging his finger and keeping the flirty women from his factory job at bay pushed him to follow through with our decision.

I took the chair after she finished with him. It felt like my appointment was with an extremely targeted bee, as each ink spot stung like one. The space between the fingers was the most sensitive part. Ink wasn't applied on the palm side, as Cindy explained, because the area was too sensitive and would wear off quickly.

My incentive was to keep my wedding rings from slipping off my finger in the cool water as I taught deep-water aerobics and swim lessons at the twelve-foot end of the YMCA's pool. My hands frequently swelled from fibromyalgia—hot and puffy, my rings practically cutting off circulation. The cool water relieved pain and swelling. I couldn't imagine having to retrieve them from the drain's grate so far below.

These tattoos became our enduring symbol of Christian covenant marriage, representing our shared intent: "until death do us part." For twenty-one happy years, we planned to grow old together, but as life changed, this symbol took on new layers of meaning.

A Visible Witness

"Miss Char, what's that on your finger?" a fourth-grade swim student asked, pointing to my inked band.

"That's my wedding band. My husband and I believe that marriage is for keeps." I smiled.

"That's rad! Did it hurt?" he asked curiously, looking it over.

"It felt like a bunch of bee stings."

"Oh!" His cringy face told me tattoos didn't appeal to him now.

They hurt too much. I hoped this would help his parents later if he considered getting one as a teen, but also that it would plant a seed for his future marriage.

A Silent Witness of Resilience

Don's tattooed ring drew admiration mixed with questions. When his coworkers learned of our commitment, their responses were exactly what we intended. The women at work stopped flirting, and the men asked about his faithfulness to one woman for life. But when Don was diagnosed with stage 4 colon cancer, our plan to grow old together grew dismal. Cancer forced us to reconsider the future, and our permanently inked bands, symbols of our faithful vows, took on a deeper meaning.

> Cancer forced us to reconsider the future, and our permanently inked bands, symbols of our faithful vows, took on a deeper meaning.

When he died in a Pittsburgh hospice center four years after his diagnosis, I touched his cold hand, gazing at his inked wedding band through tears. "Until death do us part" had come. Cancer robbed us of growing old together. I asked, *What now, Lord?*

Indelible Ink

A year after Don died, instant messaging bubbles popped up constantly: "Hey, baby!" "What a hottie!" I abruptly shut them down. I'd cautiously entered the world of adult dating. I didn't want this, but I couldn't stand being alone either. The man I mentioned earlier wasn't the only one who'd asked if I'd remove my tattooed band—it became a common question.

When I finally met God's man for me, he also asked about my

inked wedding band. When I finished sharing my story with Boaz, I heard the same question I'd heard several times before.

"I can tell you both loved each other tremendously. It must hurt knowing you wouldn't be growing old together."

"Thank you for understanding. Not everyone does."

"My Christian upbringing was strict in an old southern tradition. My family considered tattoos sinful and a sign of low self-worth. I understand you didn't get this just to turn your body into an art gallery, but would you be willing to have it removed?"

"You do realize that Don and I didn't go through a pagan temple ritual and get a tattoo to commemorate the experience? Besides, the people I know who have tattoos feel a sense of belonging, a sense of community with other people like themselves," I explained that we had thoroughly researched the Bible and commentaries to ensure we weren't doing anything contrary to our Christian faith.

"I understand, but I would feel better if it were removed."

Since he was sincere in his convictions and I felt he was likely God's man for me, I tried slow removal via microdermabrasion. Grief lingered during the process as it dragged on for months. I had other reminders of my life with Don. It seemed like just ink. But was it?

After I realized it wasn't fading, I told Boaz, "I tried, but it's not budging. Laser removal is quite expensive and painful."

> We could see that God had a great sense of humor and purpose with my tattoo.

"I can see that you gave it your best effort. Don is probably looking down from heaven, laughing!" he chuckled. We could see that God had a great sense of humor and purpose with my tattoo.

He accepted that it was part of my life. It also gave our midlife remarriage greater meaning.

After we married, my inked band still peeked out from under my titanium rings. Though removal failed, nearly thirty years of experience shaped our midlife remarriage—the ink became a mark of forever love, grief, and new beginnings. Even now, it draws attention in ordinary moments.

A Silent Witness

I sat in our car waiting in the instant oil change line for my turn. I pulled up when the lube technician waved me forward. He immediately noticed my permanent wedding band beneath my wedding rings as he held his clipboard to ask me the usual questions about my car. "What's that?" He pointed it out.

"It's a tattooed wedding band."

"What happened? If you don't mind me asking. It looks like you've been married more than once." He'd noticed that my band and name matched Boaz's, who also goes there.

I briefly shared about my tattoo and late husband, and mentioned that my Boaz and I now wear matching titanium bands.

"Yes, I've seen his. Wow! That's so cool! Thank you for your willingness to share your story. I have to tell my wife about it. We've talked about getting our wedding bands tattooed since our rings are tight now."

"Certainly, feel free to share it with her."

I never realized the significance of that simple inked ring when I laid Don to rest. Through years of marriage, Don's death, and starting over, my inked band is a silent testament to faithful, resilient love. It reminds me that Christian covenant marriage withstands many tests. The new titanium rings above them stand as a tribute to God's blessing and the strength found in enduring love.

Hope After Hurt

ALISA O'DONNELL

SOMETIMES AN EVENT HAPPENS AND catches you off guard, and yet somehow, it's not surprising at all. The year 2020 was a banner one for trauma and hardship, but it was also the year that jump-started my journey toward healing.

A family member (let's call her Sarah) was on a video call doing Bible study with my mom and me. We were wrapping things up when she confessed, "I left my husband a few weeks ago. I finally acknowledged how abusive he has been, and I need to ask for your forgiveness because I didn't protect you from him."

I was not surprised by this confession. In fact, I remembered saying years before how Sarah's husband had been emotionally and psychologically abusive. I was more surprised that she had finally admitted it and left.

I also knew that I had been mistreated in the relationship for years as well. Sarah and her husband had been parental figures to me. While I knew that his treatment was wrong and didn't reflect who I was or my worth, over the years, I just buried the mistreatment, tried to keep the peace, and ignored the ways it was really messing me up.

Once Sarah got free from the abuse, I found the freedom to acknowledge that I'd been abused too. I had lived with more than meanness or occasional hurtful comments. I had endured systematic discouragement meant to control me and others around me.

Naming the Wound

Acknowledgment led to anger. To be honest, I spoke in ways I'm not proud of about what I had been through because I was bitter, and it was the only way I could seem to take back some agency.

I thank God I was at home with my parents during that season, surrounded by their faith and love. Although my perception of God had eroded over the years, in part because of how I had been treated by someone who "loved" me, I was still seeking God. And in his great love, God challenged me, refusing to give up on me when I was broken.

> God challenged me, refusing to give up on me when I was broken.

At first, I was delighted at the thought of cutting my abuser out of my life. I had the axe at the ready and figured once I did that, I could close the door on that chapter of life.

So, when God asked me instead to pursue peace, to express forgiveness, and to offer reconciliation, I was, frankly, mad. But God saw my axe and raised me a scalpel, nudging me to take a different approach to the situation.

I was not the only one with skin in the game, so to speak, when it came to restoration or alienation. God showed me that, in this situation, other people close to me deserved a voice in the decision. But it felt unfair that I couldn't just focus on myself. I knew that I wouldn't be able to believe any apologies or professions of repentance from the one who hurt me. But I chose to let God show me a path forward.

And for a time, it played out as expected. I heard excuses, justifications, and devaluations. I got more hurt, more angry, and more upset with God. What was the point if nothing was going to change?

> What was the point if nothing was going to change?

I came to the Bible then, determined to find an answer: Are Christians allowed to walk away from toxic and harmful relationships? What does Jesus's "seventy times seven" statement in Matthew 18 mean? Do we have to take people back, regardless of repentance?

When Forgiveness Isn't Simple

My searching led me to compassion, and that's where my healing and renewal truly began. I set boundaries because I could no longer play therapist to people who needed serious professional help. In addition, I was working to forgive while trying to let my wounds be known so that they could heal. But none of it seemed to be enough. Others seemed to question my heart and my motives in every conversation.

As I began to study biblical compassion, I started to see how it made space for a fresh start—and how a fresh start wasn't a static scenario but a continuum based on situational factors.

It took work still to make a fresh start with Sarah. We had to relearn how to know each other. Sarah expressed immense guilt for how things had played out, even though most of it was not hers to carry or make amends for.

Her ex (we'll call him Gary), on the other hand, was essentially unwilling to acknowledge his behavior. Everything had a justification. Someone else had caused him to be the way he was, or so he said.

With Sarah, I could extend compassion because she was desperate for it. She showed that she longed to heal and restore what was broken. When I showed her compassion, I saw the payoff and felt the healing.

But I could not give Gary the same kind of compassion because it was not healthy or helpful. To make compassion one-size-fits-all was to enable harmful behavior and unrepentance. But to withhold it entirely was to water the root of bitterness that I was trying to eradicate. I recognized the importance of compassion, but I still found myself wondering, "How can compassion help me heal?"

Compassion with Discernment

For me, compassion first began with prayer. In those days, all I could pray was that God would get a hold of Gary's heart and do a miracle. And believe me, repentance could only come through God's active work. It would never occur otherwise. I prayed Scripture because I knew I would struggle to find genuine words on my own.

> I prayed Scripture because I knew I would struggle to find genuine words on my own.

After an attempt at communication, I next had to employ a boundary of space. I wasn't shutting the relational door, but the Lord had finally given me freedom to focus on other aspects of my healing. Forgiveness was underway, bitterness was being rooted out, and my heart was broken for the excuses that were keeping Gary from restoration with God and with others.

The final piece, and the one that is still my biggest struggle, was choosing compassionate speech. It's hard to want to speak graciously about someone who has hurt us, more so when they have not taken full responsibility. But compassion is not only a feeling to act on. It is a choice to make that guides us in resilience.

Balancing Compassion and Boundaries

The dictionary defines *resilience* as "the ability of a person to adjust to or recover readily from" adversity.* Resilience is not brushing things off or sweeping them under the rug, which I did for years. It is being ready for recovery, healing, and restoration.

Resilience, like compassion, is a choice. And if I've learned anything in recent years, it's that compassion leads me in a life of resilience. I cannot always control what happens to me. I cannot always expect the unexpected. And I don't believe I am supposed to live braced for the worst-case scenario. What I can do is prepare myself for recovery by cultivating compassion in daily life.

> Once I saw him as beloved by God, I couldn't see him any other way.

I didn't have any grace in my heart for Gary when everything finally fell apart. But through compassion, I recognized that Gary was a broken man who needed God's healing in some of the same ways that I did. Once I saw him as beloved by God, I couldn't see him any other way.

Compassion taught me to treat others as image bearers of God, no matter how they do (or don't) reflect that. It moved me beyond

---

* Dictionary.com, s.v. "resilience," accessed December 24, 2025, https://www.dictionary.com/browse/resilience.

the immediate situation to the root of the problem: surrender to our loving God. I have fought against surrendering. When I see someone doing that now, it stirs up compassion and spurs me to action. God's heart in me allows me to discern whether what I'm doing serves a heavenly good or merely an earthly one. Sometimes, what I think is compassion only touches the earthly symptom but leaves the eternal root diseased.

Sometimes compassion is distance, silence, or natural consequences. The boundaries I use to keep myself safe can challenge another person to consider why I need protection in the first place, which may lead them to self-reflection and repentance. And if it doesn't, that isn't my responsibility to carry. Compassion heals my heart so that I can move forward, no matter what happens in any particular relationship.

> Compassion heals my heart so that I can move forward.

I wanted a fresh start after enduring years of hurt, and God gave me one. I resisted for a time, but I am thankful now that God didn't let me off the hook. Through compassion, God showed me where I have agency in my own life. I do not have to carry a label of victim, with all its crutches and vices. Through compassion, I can choose resilience instead. I can find hope—not just for the future, but for right now.

A Fresh Start

I'd love to say that all the difficulties have been resolved. I'd love to say that compassion was life-changing not only for me but for Gary too. But that isn't my claim to make.

Many interactions are still difficult. I'm not always sure where I stand or what I should believe. My fight-or-flight instinct is on high alert sometimes. I regularly have to remind myself that I am committed to forgiveness and gracious speech. Because while it heals, compassion is not a magic cure. It's more like a tool I use to whittle away my old self so I can put on the character of Christ. Compassion cannot control another person, and so it can't force a relationship to be made new. Instead, as I practice compassion, it softens my heart and gives me a fresh start each day, each interaction, to walk in the spirit.

Big-Time Trouble

SUE FERGUSON

AFTER OUR PHONE CALL ENDED, Ruth's statement replayed in my mind. "I would've had no trouble putting down a dog that acted like that."

No trouble.

Ruth had read my book and knew the trauma I experienced with my youngest Goldendoodle.

My gaze went to Wilson. He slept peacefully on his back, feet sticking straight up, in a common doodle pose.

She would have had no trouble putting him down. No trouble. Putting him down.

It hurt to hear those words. *What if we had?*

I would've missed out on so much.

When things were at their worst, the thought had crossed my mind. It seemed like the only option. I'd quickly shoved the thought aside, though, because it was big-time trouble for me.

Even though Wilson proved to be more than I knew how to handle nearly every day, I loved him. When he wasn't overreacting to his fears, he was a precious companion.

Remembering the pain of that difficult season renewed my appreciation for where we are today. Reflecting on those challenging years and the many times I'd hoped for resolution only to be disappointed forced me to admit that hard times often yield growth and delight that surpass what we experience when things come easily.

During that rough season, I was desperate for normal life to resume. If I'd known someone willing to take Wilson and capable of training him, I probably would've given him away. But I doubted I could give Wilson to someone since he would act like a killer dog when they came to meet him. But, put him down? I couldn't go there. I had to find a better way.

> I couldn't go there. I had to find a better way.

After all, I paid a small fortune for him and didn't want to give up. From the day we brought him home, I'd tried to do everything perfectly. Obviously though, my attempts at perfection weren't the best for Wilson.

Though determined to work through our dreadful situation, I was clueless as to how to resolve our problem. I'd never seen a dog look so mean except on a television or iPad screen—and those dogs had been police protection dogs or criminals' accomplices—not stuffed toy-looking fluff balls adorned with colorful kerchiefs.

That was part of the problem; Wilson is adorable. He magnetically pulls children and dog-loving adults in his direction. His looks appear to say, "Let's be besties," but his actions contradict that sentiment.

Even now, Wilson likes to vet his acquaintances and then warm up to them on his own terms. But in those early days, he was more than a little frosty—more like an unexpected thunderous hailstorm.

BIG-TIME TROUBLE

Jules, the trainer I'd used with our older doodle, Einstein, had moved away. She truly loved dogs and welcomed texts and emails—happy to offer support from afar. When she returned for a visit, she offered to make a house call.

Yes, thank you.

During Jules's visit, she determined Wilson had no respect for me. It was true he didn't gaze deep into my eyes as Einstein did. He showed no desire to please anyone but himself. Jules took the leash and corrected him a few times; I didn't notice any positive results. She said, "I think he has a different personality and needs firm structure and boundaries, but there's nothing wrong with your dog."

Jules was right; there was nothing wrong with Wilson. What she didn't say, and may not have known what I now do, was that Wilson needed me to change. My communication with Wilson didn't provide the clarity and security he required. I had to change what was wrong with me before Wilson could change what seemed to be wrong with him.

> I had to change what was wrong with me before Wilson could change what seemed to be wrong with him.

After Jules's visit, I met a new-to-me local trainer. Zero help. Then I tried several online courses. Even though I tried what each one recommended, Wilson didn't respond like the perfect dogs in the videos. It was embarrassing and humiliating to have a fluffy dog who acted like he wanted to kill people.

Wilson's outbursts became more frequent. I removed him from uncomfortable situations. Unknowingly, I rewarded the behavior I wanted to eliminate because I provided an escape from his fearful encounters.

Desperate, I threw money at almost any dog training opportunity that appeared in my Facebook feed. I began to doubt whether any trainer could help with my difficult dog.

I gave up on online classes until an inexpensive course showed up on Facebook. The entire course was a short ebook on overcoming fear reactivity. From my online research I'd been able to diagnose that as the condition Wilson suffered from. Since many people spend as much on coffee every week as the cost of clicking BUY NOW, I justified my click. The brief ebook provided a breadcrumb to follow.

The author had fixed his reactive dog by learning from a trainer he'd watched on YouTube named Larry.

I need that trainer.

I found the trainer on YouTube and, after watching several of his videos, I knew he could fix Wilson. After all, he dealt with dangerous dogs—ones that were safety risks for their own families. Soon I was on his website, and shortly after I arrived there, tears streamed down my face when I read, "Most issues are more easily solved than you think. Don't give up on your dog."

We were close.

It had been two difficult years since Wilson's first angry outburst. Two years of attempting different training solutions. Two years of anxiety every time I took him outside or if someone, even family, came to visit.

I sent an email to Larry asking if we could bring Wilson to him for a *board and train.* Afterward, I checked my email every thirty minutes. A few days passed with no response; I decided to call. There was no answer, so I left a voicemail message and held on to my iPhone as if it were a lifeline. No callback.

Wilson wasn't going to a *board and train* anytime soon.

I had no idea the trainer was world-renowned. Working with aggression cases is one of his many specialties. Trainers all over the world seek opportunities to learn from him.

Finally, realization struck. *I might never hear from him.*

With determination, I went to my computer and created a DIY plan based on what I was learning from the miracle-working YouTube videos.

> My closest friends knew of my desperate situation and joined me in praying for some way to connect with him.

My closest friends knew of my desperate situation and joined me in praying for some way to connect with him. Three months later, Ellen texted me a photo she had taken of his Facebook post announcing a group class open to the first twenty people to make payment. I rushed to sign up.

Class wouldn't begin for ten long weeks, but hope made the future seem brighter.

From January to October of 2022, I attended nine group classes. And, as you might guess, in the beginning, Wilson made it easy to see and hear why we were there. Many of the classmates were trainers with well-behaved dogs. They wanted to excel further.

Wilson was a stand-out for all the wrong reasons. He lunged and killer-barked at everyone in the first class. But when the trainer took the leash from me, Wilson immediately calmed. I knew then and there we were exactly where we needed to be.

By the time the classes ended, Wilson may have been the most improved class member. Many of the others were beautifully trained to start with.

THREE YEARS HAVE PASSED SINCE those transformational classes took place. When I think of the days before those sessions, tears almost always form. As sweet as today is, I haven't forgotten the pain of those desperate days.

If someone capable of dealing appropriately with Wilson's challenges had offered to take him, I would have cried like a baby and, more than likely, handed him over. I'm glad that person didn't come along, and I'm thankful putting him down was big-time trouble for me. Because I ended up with more than a delightful dog.

The truth is, our awesome trainer didn't train Wilson. Oh, he held his leash several times and answered a million of my questions. As I watched him with each dog and their human, the humans struggled the most. Once humans get it, the dogs follow suit.

The trainer could have taken the easy way out and set the foundation for Wilson's training fast, but instead, he chose the difficult task of teaching me. In the process, I learned a lot about training Wilson and any dogs in my future. The whole process taught me a lot about myself too. I had to change so that Wilson could change.

> I had to change so that Wilson could change.

I would've never chosen the difficult path Wilson required me to take. Wilson isn't perfect, but I have a cherished, furry companion that makes me laugh every day. I'm so glad I didn't give up.

Courage When Lights Go Out

KAY NELL MILLER

AT FORTY-THREE YEARS OLD, MY husband, Phil, and I sold our twenty-year wholesale coffee roasting business to our employees, and we kicked back to relax. Our son was five years old, and we wanted to savor the time with him since we had been married eighteen years without children.

The years that followed were priceless. But suddenly, he was seventeen and leaving home for the first time to live at a fire station. As he drove out the driveway for the final time, he yelled, "Thanks for raising me!"

I walked inside, dropped to the floor sobbing. I knew my life would never be the same.

Twinkling Lights

Phil found his bliss in working in our large, thirty-year-old forest, making it a beautiful park setting day after day. I gave it a good shot out in the forest with him, and I was bored to death.

I went to a local garden club, and I didn't know a soul. Everything I had tried to grow died a quick death. However, I soon learned these were not your traditional garden club women. Still,

I'm not sure why I chose to attend the garden club, as I had no real interest in planting things, and gardening bored me as much as working in the forest day after day.

Phil and I are opposites. He's an introvert, thinker, and plodder. I am a mix between extrovert and introvert, a do-er who likes to make things happen.

> Struggling didn't even cover the way I felt after selling our business.

Struggling didn't even cover the way I felt after selling our business. Plus, all my friends were still working. Our home was way too quiet, and we were both searching for great things to fill up our time. Phil's search was over when he was working in the woods and motorcycle dirt riding on trails with his buddies.

Lest you think I just needed Jesus, he and I were tight. I was exhausted from my caregiving role for my mom (dementia raised its ugly head for thirteen years until she passed). We had wonderful times together during the thirteen years, and I learned great things about caregiving. Some the easy way. Some the hard way.

Lights Out

It was exactly one year and forty-five days past caregiving for my mom when my life changed in one second forever. Phil was heading to Central Oregon to camp out and ride dirt bike with about twenty other faith-based guys. At home, pressure washing the deck, I was praying for their travels as Phil and his nephew headed out for adventure.

Later, my best girlfriend had arrived to watch a movie when the phone rang. It had to be a spam or sales call, so answering in my most aggressive voice, I said, "Yes?"

"Hello, is this Kay Nell Miller?"

"Yes. Who's this?"

"This is the chaplain from St. Charles Hospital in Bend. Your husband had an accident and is here in the ICU."

"Let me speak to the doctor."

"He's busy working on him."

"Let me speak to the charge nurse." I knew the lingo.

"She's busy working on him."

"Well, how is he?"

"Well…"

"Is he dead?"

"No, but they're working on him. He wants you to come to Bend, but he doesn't want you to come alone."

Oh, that's not my man. That's about a four-hour drive. I knew it must be bad, as Phil would never ask me to travel four hours and *not* to come alone!

"Okay. I'm on my way."

After spinning my body in circles to get my bearings, I headed to my car.

"What do you want to do with your dog?" my best friend asked.

"I don't know. Handle it." She was good at handling things.

> I called multiple friends, but none were available.

I called multiple friends, but none were available. Finally, I thought to call my favorite nephew, and within twenty minutes, we were on our way to Bend. After dialing my son's firefighter captain, I explained the situation. One hour later, we picked him up from where he was standing in the middle of the road waiting for us.

From that moment until we would arrive home a few months later, I could feel God's presence intensely. No prayers needed by me, as we were intimate like never before, and my life was a living prayer in the following days.

On the way to Bend, I called a myriad of family and his friends. Receiving responses all the way from the unhelpful "Oh, he's going to be fine. It's not that bad" to the ones who understood: "We're on our way." My niece Heather was the only one in my family that I could reach. Later, I called to say no one needed to come until I could see Phil and know what we were dealing with.

"Too bad," I was told. "We're all on our way and halfway on the other road to Bend!" My extended family, many of the dirt bike riders, and our carload all arrived within five minutes of each other at the hospital. The neurosurgeon sauntered in, as he had just completed fusing Phil's neck, C3–C4, to relieve the swelling pressure and help him breathe.

"He has a very long road to recovery. He has no feeling from his neck down and is a quadriplegic." Clear and concise. I loved his directness.

> He was connected to monitor after monitor, wearing a huge neck brace, and lying flat.

Holding my son's hand behind my back, we slowly walked into the ICU, seeing Phil for the first time. He was connected to monitor after monitor, wearing a huge neck brace, and lying flat. His eyes were open, and I kissed his cheek. He said "Hi" and fell back to sleep.

They allowed two of us in the ICU at a time, sitting in chairs, leaning on Phil's bed rail, and praying non-stop. We were fifteen days in Bend. After he was out of intensive care but still in the hospital, I walked into his room.

"I don't want to live like this! Unplug me from all the machines, I just want to die!" he said.

Day after day, I'd heard his mantra, and I was weary and sad.

> Day after day, I'd heard his mantra, and I was weary and sad.

"I don't want to live like this! Unplug me from all the machines. I just want to die."

Sick of hearing his mantra, one day I looked around. "Phil, I think God's got a different idea. You're not plugged into any machines." And I laughed.

When the physical therapist arrived the next day, she said confidently, "We're going to head outside today."

"No, I'm not going outside. I just want to die."

"Well, we're going outside anyway."

I gave her a thumbs up behind his back. I was thrilled that she was confident and knew what he really needed.

Flickering Lights

After that day, Phil never said he wanted to die again. He started digging in, learning how to live with a severe spinal cord injury.

Lest you think it's been easy. It has not. Phil's endured multiple surgeries and recoveries, two months of in-patient spinal cord rehabilitation, and I slept on a cot there with him. He's had physical therapy, occupational therapy, recreational therapy, and the fifteen days in Bend, Oregon.

Miracles happen, even fourteen years later. Phil walks slowly with a grocery cart for thirty minutes a day, he uses a push walker to go very short distances, and is in an electric power wheelchair 95 percent of the time. He can drive with adaptive equipment in his wheelchair van. Yet he continues with no feeling below his neck.

Some people left us. Some people stayed. His cycle-riding buddy has been coming weekly for fourteen years to spend the day with him. They go to the gym, Phil runs a log splitter from his chair, and they eat at their favorite restaurant. His friend encourages him to fix things with one hand and do many other creative things. His buddy can get Phil to do things that I cannot.

Sweet, Courageous Lights

Phil and I are closer than we've ever been. What has gotten us through? Faith. Patience, even when we are worn thin. Hope. We live one day at a time and just celebrated our fifty-first anniversary. Marrying Phil was the best life decision I ever made. No regrets. All the lights are on.

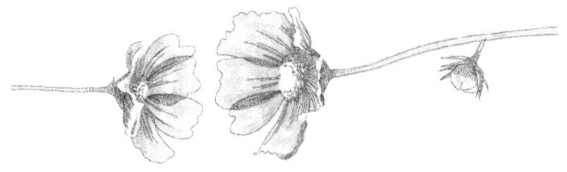

Perfectly Stationed

PAM WHITLEY TAYLOR

I WAS ONLY FIFTY-TWO WHEN MY first husband, Mike, died. Two years prior to his diagnosis, we'd moved to a new town, and our lifelong friends were miles away. The days that followed his August death seemed to bring more tears as each *first* without him overwhelmed my heart. Never had I felt so alone.

Drinking my morning coffee alone was dreadful, as was crawling into an empty bed at night. Then came his fifty-fifth birthday two months after his death. What an excruciating day of sadness that was. It took me months to realize that the life I had known was forever gone, and that was before I'd faced Thanksgiving and Christmas without him. Oh my. They were the hardest.

I cried my way through Thanksgiving, and I shopped for flowers for his newly placed headstone during the Christmas holidays. I sobbed my way through December 22, which would have been our thirty-third wedding anniversary. Then came Christmas Day, and his empty dinner chair seemed to scream, "He's not here!"

My precious daughter-in-love and son quickly turned the table in a different direction when I walked out of the room. Believe it or not, that helped us all. The chairs were in different places, and his chair no longer seemed to declare his absence!

The New Year dawned, and I received an invitation from my church to the singles' Valentine's banquet! I pondered why they'd send me an invitation—ironically, it took a bit for me to recognize my new label was *single*! More tears flowed.

Then came Easter weekend. By then it had been about six months since I'd lost Mike, and I thought I should have myself together better than I did, but I didn't.

To make matters worse, the entire week before Easter was filled with delightful spring weather, but on the Saturday morning before Easter, I awoke to the sound of the wind howling outside. I peeked through the window. A dense fog and a chilling drizzle pervaded the view as the wind mercilessly whipped the tender new buds of spring. I turned the TV to the weather channel—and the weatherman predicted a freeze that night.

Reluctantly, I shoved back my fuzzy comforter and slipped out of my warm refuge. I peeked through the window one more time and shivered as the Oklahoma winds pounded the cold rain against the glass. My spirit felt very much like the day looked—dark, cold, and dismal.

> My spirit felt very much like the day looked—dark, cold, and dismal.

I pulled my robe tightly around me and headed to the kitchen to make my morning coffee. My gaze settled on Mike's coffee cup in the cabinet as I grabbed mine. Everything was a reminder of his absence, and I dreaded Easter without him—and the empty space that would once again be beside me in tomorrow's church service. Would I ever recover from losing him?

My mind then skipped to the next day's lunch that I would prepare for my son and his family— and to the treasures I'd planned for our grandbabies' Easter baskets. The previous year, Mike had delighted in hiding Easter eggs and carving the ham. Tears welled up in my eyes again. *Oh Lord, can I ever be content without my Mike?*

I poured my cup of coffee and returned to my bedroom. Plumping the pillows against the headboard, I crawled back under the warm covers and grabbed my Bible. I turned to the psalms and opened to Psalm 22. The first verse I read touched my heart, "Lord, why are you standing aloof and far away? Why do you hide when I need you the most?"

I read it again.

I cried out, "Lord, you know I feel just like this. You seem so far from me, and I don't understand."

Though I wanted to stay in bed, I knew I'd better get ahead of the holiday crowds and buy the rest of my groceries for my Easter meal. I exchanged my Bible for a notepad and listed the remaining things I needed. Then I pulled on my jeans, grabbed my umbrella, and headed out the door.

Since we'd been empty nesters for a while, we typically went out for breakfast on Saturday mornings and then drove to Sam's Wholesale Club to shop a bit. That was one of Mike's favorite places to go. Our trip usually concluded at the Sam's gas station as Mike put gas in my car for the week. He'd insisted on pumping that gas long after brain tumors rendered him unable to drive.

Today, I thought I'd get the gasoline first since my gauge was near empty. As I pulled toward the pump area, my cell phone rang. With the distraction, I failed to see that two young people—a guy and a gal—stood beside the gas pump where I pulled in.

When I finally saw them, negative thoughts overtook me!

Oh great. Just what I need—someone who wants money to wash my windshield or is raising money for something. Maybe I can back up.

I glanced back, and two cars had already pulled in line behind me. It was too late for me to move. I fumbled through my wallet for my Sam's card and braced myself for their sales pitch as I stepped out of my car.

> I braced myself for their sales pitch as I stepped out of my car.

"Good morning." The young woman cheerfully handed me a business card that had her church's info on it.

"We're here this Easter weekend on behalf of Real Church." Her brown eyes sparkled, and her long brown hair whipped in the freezing wind as she pointed across the street to their building. "We're here to tell you that God loves you, and to fill your gas tank for free."

Surprised, I protested, "That's wonderful of you guys, but I am a Christian, and I love the Lord. I don't want you to spend your money on me. Please use it for the next car, and let me pull on through."

"No, Ma'am," came the response. "We've prayed about who is coming to our line, and you're exactly who we want to do this for."

I hesitated, but then sat back in my car, leaving my door slightly ajar. They swiped their credit card and began to pump my gas, something that had not been done for me since Mike's death. The tears started to come.

"This is so kind of you and your church," I managed to choke out through the tears.

The young man smiled and said, "Our congregation wanted to do something special this Easter for this neighborhood. One of our members had this idea and donated the money. We'll fill up tanks until the money is gone. We want to tell as many people as we can that God loves them."

I sat there in numbness as I thought back to the psalm I'd read earlier that morning when I had not wanted to get out of bed. I recalled my statement to God about feeling he was far away, and the tears once again flowed.

I looked up at the two young people and said, "I want you to know that God sent you guys to stand in my husband's shoes today." My voice quivered as I struggled to get out the rest of my words. "My husband died last fall, and this is my first Easter without him. He'd normally be pumping my gas for me. Instead, here you are, standing in his shoes. You'll never know how your sweet and caring gesture has blessed me today. Thank you, and please thank your church for me too."

"Ma'am, I'm honored to have this privilege," the young man said as his voice cracked.

> A lot more than my gas tank was filled that day as I thanked God for those two young people stationed at the gas pump.

I hugged them both before I drove away. A lot more than my gas tank was filled that day as I thanked God for those two young people stationed at the gas pump—giving out his message of "I love you." My day no longer seemed so dismal and dreary either, and I knew God wasn't hiding from me after all. Joy inched its way into my heart.

That day was truly a turning point in my grief. Yes, there were many more *firsts* still to come, but I knew I'd get through them as I learned I needed daily to remind myself of God's presence and his love when I felt so alone. And I needed to thank him for the almost thirty-three years he had blessed my life with such a good man. Thank you, Lord.

Waiting at the Window

PAULA HEMINGWAY

THOSE HAPPY DAYS OF HULA-HOOPS, hopscotch, and the hokey pokey meant that much of my childhood I rocked around the clock playing those groovy games with my three sisters and the neighborhood kids.*

Almost every day, though, my sisters and I took a break from our girlish games to play another game that didn't involve rules or equipment but was infinitely more important. Late in the afternoon, we hopped onto our living room divan, leaned against the back of the well-worn furniture, and peered through the front picture window to wait in excited anticipation for someone of more consequence to us than Shirley Temple, Elvis, or even the president of the United States. Our wait rewarded us when a bulky, dome-shaped white 1950s Buick my parents called Ole Betsy (they named everything) swung alongside the curb and stopped in front of our house. The car door opened, and out popped our hero.

---

* A version of this story appeared in *Miracles in Tough Times* (Guideposts, 2009), Mary Hollingsworth, editor.

All four of us dashed out of the house, jumping up and down like pogo sticks, yelling, "Daddy! Daddy!" Our long springy curls bounced as we raced down the path to hug and cling to his legs. He stiffly lumbered along the sidewalk, saddled with the extra cargo of four little girls, but nevertheless relishing this daily homecoming routine after a demanding day. We cared little that Dad drove a clunker car or that we lived in a downscale house or wore homemade clothes. What counted was that Dad was there. We loved our daddy.

> I thank God my daddy always came home. He never once stood us up.

I thank God my daddy always came home. He never once stood us up. His commitment to Mom and us girls, solid as our saddle shoes, provided love, security, and protection for our family and a lifetime of trust in our heavenly Father.

As I grew into an adult, though, I had no inkling how that faith and trust in God would be tested. Somewhere along my life's journey, I bargained with God that if I lived for him, then nothing bad would happen to me or my family. Oh, I didn't make such a compact consciously, nor would I have admitted it out loud, but difficult events in my life drew out what was hiding behind the curtains. This window view, unlike my childhood home's picture window, was tinted by sorrow and pain that no window cleaner could wipe away.

NOW I WASN'T A CHILD leaning against the divan; I was a seasoned adult, sitting in the passenger seat, looking out the window of my car at the beautiful spring day in Arkansas, the kind of day that calls for a picnic in the park or a stroll through the neighborhood. Such delightful diversions were not to be a part of this day. Upon arrival at our park-like destination, I saw throngs of cars and people who were either clustered in groups or standing in a long line, waiting to greet our oldest daughter, Marla, and her husband, Nathan. Although deeply touched by the presence of so many, my mind considered running away.

Instead, I got out of the car and traipsed through the crowd to thank friends and loved ones for coming. I took my seat under the tent, looked straight ahead, and stared at the tiny box in front of me. I had never seen such a small casket in my life. Caskets are supposed to be lived-a-long-life adult size, not fifty-five-days-old infant size. Our first granddaughter, Halley, lay in that surreal box, and there was nothing I could do to make it better.

> I was good at making my kids' pain go away, but I was helpless to fix this.

As a mom, I was good at making my kids' pain go away, but I was helpless to fix this. *God, what about our bargain? I'll be good, and nothing bad will happen. What about that? Huh? Are you listening?* My heart pounded like a jackhammer. My brain commanded strength and composure, but my heart yearned for an emotional tsunami. My heart won a little as a few tears fell when I looked around and saw the sadness and tears of friends and family who loved us and would fix it, too, if they could. I put my arm around Marla to comfort her. I wished I could hold her in my lap as I did when she was little and something bad happened. Everyone began to sing the profound hymn of our faith, "Great Is Thy Faithfulness." It felt as if angels surrounded us, singing in beautiful, heartfelt harmony to soothe our souls.

More tears slid down my face. Only God could keep Marla's friend from breaking down as she sang the soulful Chris Rice song "Come to Jesus." This ballad has become one of our family's favorites. It tells of a young Christian who has come to Jesus, and then, as he goes through life, he sings, falls, dances, and cries to Jesus. The last line declares the victory at the end of the believer's life when we fly to Jesus and live forever. Our precious Halley did fly to Jesus, and now she lives!

WHAT IF YOUR LIFE IMPACTED hundreds of people all over the world? What if your life strengthened the faith of others? What if your life inspired others to try harder? What if your total helplessness led others to God and prayer? What if you fulfilled God's purpose for your life? Would you not have lived a successful life? Our Halley, who couldn't move, breathe on her own, or even cry, accomplished all these things in her short fifty-five days of life. What can we accomplish in eighty or ninety *years* of life?

> Halley's short life inspired our family in many ways.

Halley's short life inspired our family in many ways. One evening, we jotted down thirty-one lessons we learned from her, such as: God loves us through his people; words and notes of encouragement provide great comfort; life is valuable and worthy no matter how it comes; sometimes we are totally dependent and have no control; there is time to fulfill God's purpose for our lives; everyone loves a baby; crying is good; and our fifteen-year-old son's question, "How can anyone pay to have their baby killed?"

Our suffering deepened fifteen months later when Marla gave birth to a little boy, Porter, who had the same unknown, unnamed condition Halley had. When our youngest daughter, Laura, heard the news, she summed it up by blurting out, "What is God doing?"

That's what we all wanted to know.

MY HUSBAND, MARK, AND I were continually amazed at Marla's and Nathan's immutable love, devotion, and commitment, not only to their babies but also to each other. Amid some of the most difficult days, Nate wrote a note to Marla to tell her there is no one else in the world he could go through this with, and he's more committed to her than ever. Even though Nathan attended medical school and needed to be in class, he chose to be there for Marla and their little ones. With the prevalence of divorce in medical school and among couples who lose a child, Marla's and Nathan's commitment to their marriage and Nathan's eventual graduation from medical school are a testament to God's grace.

> We proudly watched as Marla and Nathan made difficult decisions, handled grief, and leaned heavily on God.

We proudly watched as Marla and Nathan made difficult decisions, handled grief, and leaned heavily on God. They sought godly counsel from an older couple. Marla told Nate, "No TV!" Instead, they sat on their back porch to swing, talk, and pray. Their pastor told us that in all his years of ministry, he had never seen a young couple handle profound loss as well as Marla and Nate, and they were godly examples and blessings to so many.

Loving Halley and Porter, telling stories about their hospital experiences, and finding joy in the small things replaced anger, bitterness, forever asking *why*, and resentment toward God. The most negative comment I heard Marla say was, "This really stinks."

One day after getting the second death certificate in the mail, Marla remarked to Nate, "Halley and Porter are having a much better day than we are."

Our family's reactions to such intense sadness were not always positive and productive, of course, but we each worked to respond in ways that would bring glory to God. Mark frequently updated family and friends with encouraging emails; our high school son dedicated his basketball season to Halley; another son wrote a theme for school about God being in control; our youngest wrote notes of encouragement and spoke at her church youth group; and our daughter in college visited often to support and be a friend to Marla. With the help of my sister-in-law, I created two beautiful memory scrapbooks that honor Halley's and Porter's lives.

After our hard-learned lessons, Marla and Nate adopted Shepherd from birth. He's our red-haired miracle from God, as he fits right in with his two red-haired aunts. Before long, another gift from God arrived. Marla gave birth to Owen, born healthy—and crying. What a wonderful sound! To bring Owen home from the hospital was one of the most exciting and emotional days of my life.

But that's not the end of the blessings. Marla again gave birth to a baby girl named Marley, who, as she got older, prayed for a baby sister. Seven years later, Nathan, an obstetric physician, delivered a baby girl, Norah, whom they adopted. I thank the Giver of life for those four blessings.

NOW, NATE AND MARLA MINISTER to young moms who give birth to a child who has health problems or doesn't survive. They pray, counsel, support, empathize, and cry with the devastated parents because they have experienced the same heartbreak. Their purpose continues as they help others heal from hurt and loss.

Remember my bargain with God? Well, I realized God doesn't make deals like that. Unfortunately, we live in a sick world, and I'm not immune to it simply because I love and serve him. I often thank God that I grew up in a Christian home during those happy days, but I've discovered that there can be great joy amid great sorrow when we look for God's purpose in our lives.

> Remember my bargain with God? Well, I realized God doesn't make deals like that.

Someday I'll walk up to a big house—a mansion, actually—not on a sidewalk, but down a street of gold. And there at the window of heaven will be my heavenly Father waiting for me, and next to him will be two little ones. They'll both run out to meet me. We'll hug and cling to each other as we praise God that I, too, have arrived home.

After the Harvest

MICHELLE RAYBURN

I STOOD WHERE MERE DAYS EARLIER a sea of crimson had covered the now dry earth. Closing my eyes, I could almost feel the spray of the harvest machine mist falling upon my face as a strong, warm westerly breeze tore strands of hair from my ponytail, slapping them across my face. The aroma of swamp water and rich black peat had become comfortably familiar over the preceding weeks, and it finally drew me back to where I stood.

Resting my arm on my pitchfork handle, I surveyed the recessed bog that nurtured the fruit from mere blossoms to green berries and ultimately to ripe crimson cranberries waiting for harvest.

On this day, the harvest was complete, and the vines lay brown and empty, receding into dormancy for the approaching winter months. In the spring, the cycle would begin again. My role as a temporary harvest worker was nearly complete for the year, and the fun money account was sufficiently replenished for Christmas shopping.

During the harvest, workers like me had pulled out the thirty-foot aluminum irrigation pipes from the fields and tossed them up on the banks. Then the full-time managers flooded the bogs with water from reservoirs to get the water just above the tips of the vines.

My husband was one of those guys, and he drove a machine that gently churned the berries to pluck them from the vines. The hollow cranberries floated on the surface of the water until they were corralled toward the harvest machine with floating plastic booms. The harvest crew pushed the berries toward an elevator that took them to the top where the machine rinsed them and then loaded the fruit onto trucks to haul the crop to the plant for processing.

When the Field Empties

Once the bog was harvested, the water could be let out to be reused in another bog somewhere amid the thousands of acres of berries awaiting harvest.

The harvest process of tore at some of the weaker vines and overgrowth, and clumps of detached foliage floated in the water. After the waters receded, the clumps of dead vines came to rest like rafts upon the bogs.

On this day, it was my job to collect the vine rafts with a pitchfork and haul them away to the compost pile. If left there, the dead clumps would insulate and prevent the plants from entering their dormant stage. In fact, they might actually cause the vines to begin to grow out of season. When the winter winds arrived, the growing patches of plants would freeze, and come spring, they would leave nothing but dead spots.

Break was over. Time to get back to work.

When Seasons Change

So often, creation points me to spiritual lessons.

I lived a large portion of my life thinking about spiritual growth in terms of rules, boiling it down to an equation like this: remove the pride, anger, selfishness, and impatience from your life, or it will kill the fruit. There is truth in there, and it isn't entirely unbiblical. However, it's missing a significant perspective.

Just as the harvest is only one phase of the growing season, there are important repeat practices for producing good fruit. And when one harvest is complete, there is more fruit yet to grow.

> So much of what I've produced over the years that looked like growth wasn't.

The "don'ts" sound similar to handling weeds and doing pest management. Necessary, but not the only priority for fruit growers. Too often, religiosity leans toward lists of rules that can become the sole focus of living. However, the goal of growing anything is the fruit. And so much of what I've produced over the years that looked like growth wasn't. Many of the practices I made into habits missed the point.

A plant with a lot of foliage looks healthy. But if it has no fruit, what is it?

From a young age, I thought the way to fortify myself for resilience was to immerse myself in church. We were there whenever the doors were open. I continued that practice as an adult. As a young mom, I signed up to teach Sunday school, direct VBS, lead worship, accompany the choir, and serve in women's ministry. I was also the treasurer and the custodian. I think there was one point where I did all of those at the same time. In between, I attended a Bible study and volunteered at my children's school.

A calendar packed with meetings and commitments makes me feel important. Needed. But busyness mostly produces foliage, not fruit. It might *feel* as if we're doing a lot of good, but the main fruit I reaped was exhaustion. And exhaustion leads me to be short with my family, snippy with my husband, and just plain annoying to be around.

This isn't a "worldly" problem, as some of my Christian friends might want to label it. Frankly, a lot of my busyness and overcommitment happened in that tight circle of church—in the place that was supposed to help me grow. It's easy inside that bubble to serve here, fellowship there, and find yourself occupied everywhere—every day of the week. But that doesn't mean spiritual growth happens.

> If none of it produces what Jesus is looking for, it isn't good growth.

Piling up a heap of knowledge about the Bible or logging years in the faith can look like maturity, but if none of it produces what Jesus is looking for, it isn't good growth.

So, what is the fruit?

When Love Appears

A lot of the cranberry growing season involved watering and waiting around for six months. A lot of our spiritual growth involves staying connected to Jesus (who calls himself the vine in John 15), relying on him as our source of everything. Then, the fruit begins to appear.

Is that fruit rule-keeping? No.

Is it zeal, or passion, or emotion? No.

A great spiritual vocabulary, then? No.

Jesus told his disciples that the fruit is love.*

He warned his dearest friends that trouble would come. But he called them to remain connected to him. And then, he modeled

---

* John 15:16–17

that love, praying not only for those friends but also for us. Yes. He specifically prayed for you and for me, for all who would ever believe in him in the future.[†] He prayed that we would "experience such perfect unity" that the world would recognize that God the Father had sent him—the Father who loves us as much as he loves Jesus.[‡]

> When it grows abundantly, the fruit bears witness without words.

When love shows up, everyone notices. It's unmistakable. Like cranberries floating in a brilliant sea of red at harvest, love is stunningly beautiful. When it grows abundantly, the fruit bears witness without words.

I want God to cultivate that kind of love in me, the kind that doesn't evaporate when I feel impatient, tired, worn thin. I practice it imperfectly, drawing strength from Jesus and letting that love grow, season after season.

I can't think of a better way to close this book than with the words of the apostle Paul, who described this fruit so clearly and honestly. The kind of love that never quits—the fruit that endures—is the art of resilience.

> If I could speak all the languages of earth and of angels, but didn't love others, I would only be a noisy gong or a clanging cymbal. If I had the gift of prophecy, and if I understood all of God's secret plans and possessed all knowledge, and if I had such faith that I could move

---
[†] John 17:20
[‡] John 17:21

mountains, but didn't love others, I would be nothing. If I gave everything I have to the poor and even sacrificed my body, I could boast about it; but if I didn't love others, I would have gained nothing.

Love is patient and kind. Love is not jealous or boastful or proud or rude. It does not demand its own way. It is not irritable, and it keeps no record of being wronged. It does not rejoice about injustice but rejoices whenever the truth wins out. Love never gives up, never loses faith, is always hopeful, and endures through every circumstance.

Prophecy and speaking in unknown languages and special knowledge will become useless. But love will last forever! Now our knowledge is partial and incomplete, and even the gift of prophecy reveals only part of the whole picture! But when the time of perfection comes, these partial things will become useless.

When I was a child, I spoke and thought and reasoned as a child. But when I grew up, I put away childish things. Now we see things imperfectly, like puzzling reflections in a mirror, but then we will see everything with perfect clarity. All that I know now is partial and incomplete, but then I will know everything completely, just as God now knows me completely.

Three things will last forever—faith, hope, and love—and the greatest of these is love.

1 CORINTHIANS 13

About the Contributors

ALISA O'DONNELL is a wife, mother, and Christian writer. She is using her life experiences to encourage other women to find healing and hope through biblical compassion. She is a member of Compel Pro Writers Training and has been published on several websites, including The Grit and Grace Project and Candidly Christian. When she isn't writing, she enjoys getting outside with her daughter, reading, and drinking good coffee. Connect with her at: **alisaodonnellauthor.wordpress.com**

ALMIRA MICHELE ROBINSON is a survivor of two different cancers who loves God, testifying to his goodness, and teaching the Bible. A mother of two children with a BS in Psychology and Religion who relishes her quiet time and journaling. An introvert at heart, she loves people, a good puzzle, a mystery, reading, sewing, and nature. She collects hearts, loves trees, and has moved more than the children of Israel following Jesus.

ANDREA GRIBBLE'S passion is helping schools recognize their daily awesomeness and sharing that story with the world. She's built a team that celebrates hundreds of schools across the country! #SocialSchool4EDU provides full social media management and runs a vibrant online community that provides ongoing professional development for school social media champions. She is the author of *Social Media for Schools: Proven Storytelling Strategies & Ideas for Celebrating Your Students & Staff—While Keeping Your Sanity.*

ANDREA M. POLNASZEK is a licensed clinical social worker, filmmaker, producer, screenwriter, and author whose multifaceted career glorifies God. Holding degrees from Gordon College and Southern Baptist Theological Seminary, she owns a clinical practice and authored the internationally translated "Elijah Project" series, inspiring workshops by 500 mentors in Cuba. With her sister as Boylan Sisters, she produces award-winning faith-based films, promoting mental wellness, including *Wish for Christmas* and *Switched*. Proud mother of three, she enjoys walks around Lake Wissota with husband Perry.

BROOKE R. HACKMAN deeply desires to bring validation to those personally affected by difficult circumstances, as well as a sense of connection and perspective to all her creative endeavors. Brooke has a BA in Electronic Broadcast Journalism from Washburn University. She is also the social media and communications coordinator for her church's local adoption and foster care ministry, a freelance writer, blogger, and marketing copywriter. She is married and has three beautiful children.

CHARLAINE MARTIN finds joy helping women discover God's adventures in everyday life. She loves cycling on local bike trails, gardening, flying with her Boaz, and sharing tickle bugs with their grandchildren. She is a contributing writer at Crossmap.com, a contributing author in the WordGirls collective series and in *Renewed Christmas Blessings*, and author of *Twice Blessed: Learning to Live and Love Again*. You can connect with her at **charlainemartin.com**.

CRYSTAL STALLMAN lives in Iowa with her husband and two children and teaches English at the college level. She is the author of a published poetry collection and is currently working on a novel and a second poetry collection shaped by faith and family history. In her free time, she enjoys gardening, crafting, and selling her handmade work at farmers' markets and vendor events.

DIANA LEAGH MATTHEWS weaves together the past, present, and future to help women find hope and redemption through their pain. She shares her love of Christ and history through drama, music, and storytelling and is the author of *Carol of the Rooms* and *Forever Changed*. Diana lives in upstate South Carolina with her spunky Maltese, Bentley.

ABOUT THE CONTRIBUTORS

HEATHER VOGLER, along with her husband of over twenty years, lives in the foothills of the Blue Ridge Mountains. With two homeschool graduates and three at home, Heather is the founder of Thrift Schooling and Thrift Steading, where she teaches her children and others how to homeschool and homestead on a budget. Heather holds a BA in Christian Education and has been featured in numerous publications. Visit Heather at **Thriftschooling.com**.

JONI TOPPER, known as the GloryTeller, shares God's glory with her compelling storytelling. A Granna, author, worship leader, speaker, and cofounder of Uprooted Women, an annual women's event, she radiates joy and passion for "being" the church. Her award-winning debut book, *The Power of a Well-Placed Yes,* highlights God's faithfulness in a small church. Joni loves encouraging others in their faith walk. **jonitopper.com**

KATHY CARLTON WILLIS is a writer and speaker known for her signature blend of whimsy and wisdom. Many refer to her as God's Grin Gal, recognizing her empathy and encouragement for those walking through hard seasons. With a Bible degree, she brings depth and clarity through her teachings. Kathy models resilient hope and hard-won authenticity for women, churches, and writers. Check out her Grin Gal line of books, her Substack, and her website: **kathycarltonwillis.com**.

KAY NELL MILLER will touch your heart with the things she has personally experienced as a caregiver, daughter, and wife. She opens the gates of courage and strength and shares from firsthand experience how love and life can be good even in the worse situations. She is the author of two books full of inspiration, encouragement, and hope. Kay Nell has been a full-time caregiver for decades as well as owning a business. **kaynellmiller.life**

KELLY WILSON MIZE is a wife, mother of two young adults, and adoring cat mom with twenty-five years of experience as a published author. A former educator with a master's degree in education, she has written numerous stories, devotions, and curriculum projects for publishers including Lifeway, Bethany House, and Guideposts. Her first picture book, *The Beautiful Story Within Me*, released in 2021, with another soon to follow.

LISA-ANNE WOOLDRIDGE is inspired by illuminated manuscripts and stained-glass windows. Her heartwarming true stories have been published in several popular collections. Her second novel, *The Cozy Cat Bookstore Mysteries—The Rose and Crown*, is now available online. She lives in the land of mountains and valleys that drink in the rain of heaven—otherwise known as Oregon, or you may find her at **Lisa-Anne.net**.

LISA L. CROWE is a writer, a reader, a dog lover, and a fountain pen enthusiast. She serves as prayer team director for her local church and leads a ladies' Bible study. Lisa loves to travel, read, and hike the beautiful Appalachian Mountains. She shares her Canton, NC, home with her two dogs, Daisy and Bernie. You can connect with Lisa on Facebook or Instagram, where she microblogs. Find **@LLCrowe66** on Facebook.

LORI VOBER is a survivor, overcomer, connector, and encourager. She suffered a hemorrhagic stroke at age twenty-nine and then developed epilepsy from the stroke. Lori is passionate about choices, and even in our trials, we can still find hope, joy, and new success. Even with her difficulties, Lori and her husband, Dainis, were able to become adoptive parents to a sibling group of three. Lori's journey and books can be found at **lorivober.com**.

MARTHA KNIGHT lives in the mountains of North Carolina with her husband of twenty-five years. She enjoys helping her clients organize their messy homes and watching *COPS* on TV. Martha is active in her church and especially likes to work with homeless people. Her son and daughter have made her very happy to be a grandma.

MAUREEN MILLER is an author with stories in numerous collaboratives. She contributes to Guideposts' *All God's Creatures*, her local newspaper, and several online devotion sites. Married for thirty-six years to her childhood sweetheart, Bill, they live on Selah Farm, a hobby homestead nestled in the mountains of western North Carolina. She blogs at *Windows and Wallflowers* (**maureenmillerauthor.com**)—telling of God's extraordinary character in the ordinary of life. Her debut novel, *Gideon's Book*, is now available.

ABOUT THE CONTRIBUTORS

MEL TAVARES is an award-winning author of books, articles, devotionals, and short stories. She is the acquisitions and managing editor of *Arise Daily*. Mel is also the recipient of the Advanced Writers and Speakers Association (AWSA) 2025 National Member of the Year award, holds a Doctor of Ministry in Pastoral Care and Counseling, and is a frequent event speaker and media guest. Resources can be found on her website: **DrMelTavares.com**

PAM WHITLEY TAYLOR is a wife, mother, and grandmother. She was a speaker for Christian Women's Club for many years. Both her testimony and writings share the tools she found to fight for hope, contentment, and joy in the midst of much heartache and grief. Look for her book *God's Grace Keeps Pace* on Amazon. She lives in Oklahoma and spends her days with her sweet husband of fourteen years. They enjoy photography and travel.

PAULA HEMINGWAY, married to Mark for fifty years, raised six children and is now Grammie to twenty grandchildren. Paula's stories have been published in three *Guidepost*s books, *Mature Living Magazine, The One Year Devotional of Joy and Laughter,* and *Whiskers, Wags, and Woofs.* She's a *Maxwell Leadership Certified Team* speaker, trainer, and coach. Her strong pro-life advocacy for unborn babies has led her to adopt her life slogan "Servant for Life."

SUE FERGUSON is the author of the recently released book, *Doodle Desperation: Finding My Place While Teaching The Dogs Theirs.* A perpetual learner, Sue puts all her energy into each life venture and loves to share what she learns with others. Sue is a pastor's wife, married to Randy Ferguson, nearly fifty years. Their three adult children and their spouses have blessed them with fourteen grandchildren. Visit Sue at **thesueferguson.com**.

TASHA SCHUH is a resilience speaker, author, and coach dedicated to helping others thrive despite life's unexpected challenges. After a theater accident left her paralyzed at sixteen, she went on to receive multiple honors, including the National Rehabilitation Champion Award. She has authored two books—*My Last Step Backward* and *My Next Move Forward*—and shares her message of resilience with audiences nationwide. Learn more at **TashaSchuh.com**.

Editor in Chief:

MICHELLE RAYBURN, blends humor and biblical insight to inspire audiences seeking hope in life's challenges. She is the author of more than twelve Christian living books and Bible studies, including the Selah Awards finalist *Renewed* women's Bible study, the Golden Scroll and Christian Market Awards winner *Classic Marriage,* and several award-winning anthologies. She podcasts and blogs on Substack at *Midlife Repurposed.* Married to her high school sweetheart for thirty-six years, Michelle is a proud mom of two grown sons and enjoys snuggles with her six grandchildren When she needs to reset and refocus, you'll find her in a hammock with a good book, an iced coffee, and a stash of dark chocolate. Discover more at **michellerayburn.com**.

If you have enjoyed this book, look for other collections at
FCLBooks.com